IT
WH

A FUNNY, HAPPY,
LOVING LOOK AT LIFE

Today, life isn't as simple as it once was. Problems like telephone bugs and wire taps, political scandals and the high cost of living could get a fellow really uptight. These are not laughing matters. But I've discovered that when I face them with a smile they seem to be a lot less complex. Living doesn't really cause much pain at all; it only hurts when I frown.

GROWTH UNLIMITED INC.

Dedicated to creating positive living concepts

Art Fettig, President
36 Fairview, Battle Creek, Michigan 49017
Toll Free 1-800-441-7676
616-965-2229 Fax: 616-965-4522

Originally Published by Copyright© 1973,
Liguori Publications
First Printing / November 1973

Printed in U.S.A.

Revised Edition

Revised Edition

Published by

GROWTH UNLIMITED INC.

Dedicated to creating positive living concepts

Art Fettig, President
36 Fairview, Battle Creek, Michigan 49017
Toll Free 1-800-441-7676
616-965-2229 Fax: 616-965-4522

DEDICATION

To the people who taught me to laugh . . . my mom and dad, my wife and children, Father Skiffington, Dr. Herb True and John Burdakin.

Manufactured in the United States of America

Typesetting by Insta-Print Services, Inc.

Library of Congress Catalog Number 86-081727
Fettig, Art
It Only Hurts When I Frown

ISBN 0-916927-03-2

Contents

About the author:

ART FETTIG, C.S.P.

Designated a "Certified Speaking Professional" by National Speakers Association in 1980, Art speaks for over a hundred audiences each year. His clients include General Cassett, General Foods, General Motors, General Dynamics, General Telephone and generally most of the major corporations and associations in America. He is a popular convention keynoter, banquet speaker and he offers a wide variety of seminars on Sales, Management, Safety, Wellness and Personal Growth. He also speaks for children of all ages.

Art Fettig is the father of four children, he has five grandchildren. He and his wife, Ruthie, recently celebrated their 35th wedding anniversary.

Publisher and founder of Growth Unlimited Inc., a firm dedicated to bringing positive living values to children, Fettig currently serves as president and chief executive officer of the organization.

Fettig is the author of many best selling books, booklets, audio-visual products and his varied background in sales, motivation and creativity qualifies him to custom built exciting, result producing presentations to meet your exact meeting goals.

Art may be contacted at Growth Unlimited Inc., 36 Fairview, Battle Creek, MI 49017, Toll Free 1-800-441-7676, 616-965-2229 or Fax: 616-965-4522.

Books by Art Fettig, C.S.P.

• Pos Parenting - A guide to greatness • Mentor-Secrets of the Ages • How To Hold An Audience In The Hollow Of Your Hand • Como Meterse Al Publico En El Bolsillo (Spain) • It Only Hurts When I Frown • How Funny Are You - The Humor Game (with Dr. Herb True Ph.D.) • Selling Lucky • Selling Luckier Yet • Anatomy of a Speech • Unfit for Glory • The Platinum Rule • World's Greatest Safety Meeting Idea Book • World's Greatest Sales Meeting Idea Book

PLUS: The Three Robots Series of books, activity books and tapes for children.

"Happiness Is Closin' Your Eyes"

When I was a small boy, we lived in a neighborhood where most of the boys were three or four years older than I. We played games like "Kick the can" or touch football, and I was always the one to get run over by the bigger boys, or to be sent flying on the cement with skinned hands and knees.

We had a wonderful neighbor who lived alone and had no children of her own. She'd sit on her porch on warm summer evenings and watch us. On more than one occasion she comforted me when I'd been knocked around more than usual.

"Art," she'd say, as embarrassing tears rolled down my cheeks, "you're only eight years old, but I think you are old enough to start acting like a man. Whenever you feel the tears a comin', just close your eyes and think about something wonderful you've got."

Then she would help me remember. She would remind me about the new bicycle I had received for Christmas, and that "A" I had earned in reading, and about my wonderful parents.

"Never forget, Art," she said one evening, "happiness is closin' your eyes and figurin' out what you've got to thank God about."

Today's communication media constantly dump the world's problems in our laps. Wars, riots, strikes, starvation, rising prices — you can't watch or read the news without encountering new threats to man's existence. Trouble seems to be always mounting.

Crime rates are soaring. Drug abuse threatens the health of thousands. There are more people with mental problems than ever before. Traffic and industrial accidents are on the rise. The average person's happiness quotient has decreased in inverse proportion to his affluence. So how are we to live in today's world?

These past few weeks I've thought back to the days of my youth, and I have been practicing that lesson taught to me by that kind lady who lived next door. I'm devoting time each day to the simple act of closing my eyes and thinking about something wonderful.

I think of a safer, healthier world. I think about things which I somehow haven't noticed before. I think about our recreational facilities — our beaches, our highways, our parks. I think about our schools, our beautiful churches.

I think about the food I'm able to buy; and although I gripe about my taxes and the high cost of living, I must admit I eat as well as anyone I know.

I open my eyes and look at my four children and the good health God has given them. I look at my loving wife, our comfortable home, our new carpet, our color TV, our modern appliances, and know I'm

fortunate.

I look at all this and wonder how I can be so up-tight with the world when God is treating me like this.

Why don't you try spending some time each evening with your eyes closed, counting your blessings and thanking God for them? Try thinking happy thoughts. Do like our Oriental friends do: "Count your blessings every day and learn to enjoy what you have. Imagine a world full of peace and happiness."

And one more thing. Do a little something every day to make this a happier, better world for somebody else. Extend yourself. Comfort that kid who was knocked down by the bigger boys. Encourage that fellow who's been looking for a job. Point out the good things your community leaders do and call it to the attention of other citizens.

Happiness is just closin' your eyes and seein' how wonderful life really is!

Small TALK

Amy, my two-year-old daughter, is — how do you say it? — going through a stage. In fact, I guess, to be absolutely truthful, my children have always been going through stages. I notice this especially when my wife happens to be away for the night.

On one such occasion, Amy and I began the evening with the following conversation:

"Amy," I asked, "do you like daddy?"

"No," she said.

"What did you do today, Amy, play?"

"No," she replied.

Maybe I'm doing this wrong, I thought. I'll try another approach. "You are a nice girl, aren't you, Amy?"

"No."

I scratched my head and tried again. "You are bad, then?"

"No."

"Do you want to go to bed?"

"No."

"Amy, if you don't stop that, daddy will go talk to your brother, Daniel."

"Bye-bye, daddy," Amy said.

So what does a two-year-old kid know about carrying on a conversation, I decided. Now Daniel, he's three and, besides, he's a boy and it stands to reason that a father can carry on a much better conversation with a boy than a girl. Right? Well, that is what I thought and here is how my conversation with Daniel went:

"Daddy," Daniel said, "I wanna thee wot you got."

"It's just some shaving cream, Dan."

"I wanna thee."

"Then see," I said.

"I want thum candy."

"No candy. You mother tells me you didn't finish your supper."

"Thum gum?"

"No gum. Now come over here, Dan, and get your pajamas on."

"I wanna thtay up."

"Now, Dan. You hit Amy and you are tired. So up to bed."

"I wanna watch televidgion."

"It's too late, Dan. Up to bed."

"I wanna piggyback ride."

"O.K. Get on my back."

"No. That's a horthyback ride. I wanna piggyback ride on your shoulders."

"Get on then. Now stop that . . . You're choking me," I gasped. "There now. Into bed with you and not another word."

"I've gotta go potty," he whispered.

"Well, go ahead. But come right back upstairs."

"I went potty, daddy."

"That's fine. Now under the covers with you."

"I wanna hear a thtory."

"It's too late, Dan. Now go to sleep."

Walking down the stairs, I heard: "I wanna drink."

"Come get your drink," I replied. "Now when you are all tucked in, I'll turn out the light."

"O.K., daddy. I'm ready."

I turned off the light and went into the living room to sit down when I heard his bloody cry: "Daddy, you forgot to kith me."

I jogged back upstairs and kissed him.

"And a hug," he said.

I hugged him, and gave him an extra kiss.

"Good night," he said. "Thleep tight."

Two down, and four-year-old Nancy still to go. Nancy reminds me of a teenager. It isn't that she is so big or anything, but people say that daughters are the most costly and the most trouble when they are teenagers. Somehow Nancy gives me the impression that she is most troublesome and the most costly right now.

I wonder what she'll be like when she gets to be a teenager? Maybe I'll never know. I might be confined to the poor-house by then.

Anyway, I spotted her working on one of her fleet of dolls. I think she was playing with the one that doesn't do anything but sit there. Honestly, I couldn't resist that doll when I saw it in the toy shop. It didn't wet, didn't talk, didn't walk, didn't roll over. Nothing. It just sat there like dolls used to do 50 years ago. I got so excited when I saw it, I had to buy it for her.

"How are you tonight, Nancy?" I asked.

"What did you bring me?" she asked, as she grabbed my leg when I entered the kitchen.

"I didn't bring you anything, Nancy. Daddy can't bring you something every night."

"I don't like you any more, daddy," she said.

"That's no way to talk."

"You didn't bring me nothin', so I don't like you, daddy."

"I didn't bring you *anything,* Nancy."

"I know. That's why I don't like you."

"That is a shame because daddy was going to tell you a story tonight," I said.

"I like you, daddy."

After one story, she said, "tell me another story, daddy."

"No more. That is all tonight."

"I don't like you any more, daddy."

"Now get into your nightgown and I'll carry you up to bed. O.K., honey?"

"O.K., daddy," she said. "And I love you."

I tucked her in and said, "Good night, sweety. Go right to sleep now."

"Leave the light on, daddy," she called.

"I have to turn the light off so you can sleep."

"I don't like you any more, daddy."

"Maybe it's just as well, Nancy. Goodnight."

"Goodnight, everyone," I called up the stairs.

"No," Amy replied.

"Thleep tight," Daniel called.

"I love you, daddy," Nancy answered.

I flopped down into my easy chair and just as suddenly jumped up. Daniel had left his dump truck in my chair. I removed it patiently and sat back down.

They are only going through stages, I told myself. Then I relaxed and mellowed a bit. Stages, I thought. Yes, I guess they are all going through stages, and so am I.

I'm going through the stage of fatherhood. It's hell sometimes, but most of the time it's wonderful. Like when the kids hug and kiss me and yell down the stairs like they just did.

Yes, I'm going through stages and it is great. Just great, talking to my kids like that.

That Red - Eyed Monster - The Parking Meter

Possibly you saw me running full speed down one of our mid-town streets this morning — wild-eyed, frustrated, over-excited. I'd just been victimized by that winking red-eyed monster called the parking meter.

Throughout America people are running from here to there without time to think, simply because our city fathers have found a get-rich-quick scheme for the local tax needs. And do you know what they buy with the income from parking meters? More parking meters, improved parking meters that take quarters instead of nickels. Of course, they also pay the salaries of those ever-present meter men and meter maids.

My prediction for 1975 is a graduated parking rate — possibly 10 percent of what you spend or earn while parked. Parking meters will be manned personally by certified accountants who will help you make out the necessary forms. Needless to say, they will not have the correct change; and you'll no doubt receive a summons while running in to get a fifty-dollar bill broken into fives.

Even today, the meters have me baffled. I have a little coin rack built into my car. First, it held just pennies. Then when prices went up, I had the rack changed to hold pennies and nickels. Next, the cost rose to a dime; and now I have my coin rack built to hold pennies, nickels, dimes and quarters.

Even with my coin rack, I'm usally caught with a short supply. There is something sinister about asking passers-by for change. They look at you as if, at last, they have personally encountered the mystery mugger. If they are still civilized enough to look in their pockets for the right change, it is seldom there, and you usually end up giving a total stranger two quarters for those magic four dimes in his pocket. Better to lose the 10 cents than pay a parking fine.

One alternative is a challenging game called "Find an Unexpired Meter." But the odds against winning are about the same these days as those in the game called "Find an Unexpired Civil War Veteran." To find an unexpired meter, you drive around the city with your eyes peeled on the dials of the parking meters you pass. The biggest obstacles to this are civilians on foot and suddenly stopping autos ahead of you. Sometimes, you are blocks away from your destination before you find a spot that has a few minutes left on the meter. You can't possibly run to your destination and be back in time. You can, however, use the unexpired time in playing another game — running into a nearby store and seeking the proper change. Most clerks in areas near parking meters are trained to continue their personal conversations with friends whenever a desperate parking-meter patron enters the store. They seem to have uncanny timing which seldom fails to delay you long after that ticket-writing monster has come and struck.

Not satisfied with the frustration caused by simple parking meters, our civic fathers have united in an even more sinister conspiracy. They have denoted certain parking locations as special parking zones. Here they have erected clever signs that read like this: "Loading zone. No parking between 7:00 a.m. and 12 noon, or between 4:00 p.m. and 8:00 p.m., except Sundays or holidays." What I do when I get in a spot like that is pull into the slot and consult my watch and/or my calendar. If everything is in order, then I start searching for the proper change. On finding the change, and inner voice often warns me to beware. I ignore it, feed the meter, attend my meeting and, nine times out of ten, have a ticket on my window when I return. Sometimes I get jolly little consolation notes from the enforcer. One read, "Sorry, this is just a state holiday. The sign means national holidays."

Did you ever see those little canvas covers (inscribed "No Parking") that are slipped over certain parking meters? One day, I noticed some of these in the banking areas. I suspect that whenever a bank feels there might be a run on it, they eliminate the threat by eliminating the parking. Ingenious idea: "If they can't park, they can't panic."

One afternoon recently, after running two full blocks back to my meter, I spotted one of those neatly dressed monsters they lightly call meter maids in some sections of the country. She was standing at my car's meter; and my time was down to the last minute. She had her book of tickets and her pencil in hand and was bent down urging that meter to flop over into the expired column. She was actually cheering that thing, like an excited fan at a horse race or something.

"Oh, you're back," she said brightly. "I was afraid I would have to give you a ticket."

I looked over her shoulder. "You already had it made out before it even expired. I caught you red-handed."

She blushed. "I'll tear it up," she said. "It wasn't really expired yet."

I wondered what I could do about it. Couldn't she be ticketed for sadism or something?

A plan came to mind. I put another coin in my meter and followed her along as she approached another meter. It had two minutes to go. I waited; and just as it was about to flip over, I dropped a coin in it. "You can't do that," she said. "That isn't your car."

"Try to stop me," I snarled.

She walked further down the street and I followed. She approached an expired meter, and I ran ahead of her and put a coin in. We continued this way down the block; and soon I was running out of coins. A young lad approached; I gave him a $10 bill and sent him running ahead for more change. We went two blocks like that, crossed the street and circled back. When we neared my car again, I crossed the street to put another coin in. Finally, she abandoned the area and went her merry way. I'd saved a full dozen of my fellow human beings from her sadistic devices.

I whistled as I skipped happily back to my car. It was a war, only a minor battle, true, but for once I'd won. I had developed a new tactic; and now I could spread the word around to my fellow troops. "Run ahead of those meter maids and pay the other guy's meter. What's a few cents or dollars when you can experience the intense joy of getting even? Fill the world with frustrated parking-ticket pushers."

I know it has been a long, though, losing fight for all of us. Some may have seriously considered surrender, but now we have a chance, a hope, a new method of defense and attack. If we go out there and give it the old motorist's try, we can win.

Think of the joy, the deep personal pride we can all feel once again when we can park our car and do our business, secure in the thought that down there in the street we have a fellow human being helping us in our bloody personal battle with that cruel, vicious parking meter.

Whose Homework?

Home at last. Home from a tough, trying day at the office. A day of problems. A day of driving through that pouring rain and listening to complaints and . . . I'll sure be glad when we bring Ruth home from the hospital.

Nancy, our oldest, greeted me: "Hurrah, dad is home. Can you help me with my homework?"

"Let me get in the house first," I insisted.

"It's something called approximation-rounding. I don't get it. We've got two whole pages and I have to get it done before supper because I'm going to the Campfire Girls' fashion show."

"I wanted to work on the lawn mower before dinner," I pleaded.

I went to hang up my jacket, and Daniel showed me his homework. "I have to look up these words in the dictionary and this darn dictionary doesn't have any of the words I'm looking for."

Daniel had our Concise Edition of Webster's instead of his children's dictionary, and the words he was searching for were *gole, herican, brese* and *gussed.* He had to look them up and find a brief definition. I was about to respell his words so that he could start over when Nancy called me again, "Come on, dad. Let's get this done."

Amy spotted me. "Hi, dad," she said. "Will you help me with my spelling? I have 10 words to learn and I have to learn them tonight."

"Later," I said.

"Have you got them?" Daniel asked.

"Come on, dad," Nancy called.

"Look up this word, Daniel . . . G-A-L-E," I said.

"That's supposed to be G-O-L-E," Daniel corrected.

"No, Daniel," I said, "that is why you can't find it in the dictionary. You spelled it wrong."

"That is the way the teacher spelled it on the board," he argued.

"Just look up G-A-L-E," I insisted. "And use this children's dictionary."

I walked into the kitchen where Nancy sat looking completely mystified. "Approximation-rounding," she said, "I don't get it."

I studied the example and I didn't get it. I studied it again, and suddenly it made sense. "Simple, Nancy," I said. "You just round the numbers off. If they ask you to round the number off to the nearest 10, then you drop the last number and go up or down on the second from the last. If they ask you to round it off to the nearest thousand, then drop the last three numbers and go up or down on the fourth from the last."

"Huh?" Nancy said.

"I've got 10 words to learn for spelling," Amy said.

"I found it," Daniel called.

"What's it say?"

"Very strong wind."

"Write it down."

"I lost it."

"Find it again, and write it down."

"Ten words," Amy said.

"Go study them."

"I already did. I want you to hear them."

"Not now, Amy. Go study them and I'll hear them later."

"Come on, dad," Nancy said, "I don't understand this."

"What?"

"Approximation-rounding."

David, age six spotted me as he came bounding down the stairs. "Did you bring me anything?" he asked

"Did you bring *me* anything?" I countered..

"No," he said, "just my papers from school." Proudly, he brought me a paper. It was his drawing of a purple-orange wagon and three idiotic kids standing nearby with their arms outstretched like they were attending a fanatic religious revival.

"How nice."

"Sign it."

"Sign it?"

"The teacher wants to know you saw my work," he said.

I signed it.

"Ten words," Amy said.

"I got it," Daniel called fromt the living room. "What now?"

"Later, Amy. Daniel, now look up the word H-U-R-R-I-C-A-N-E."

"That's H-E-R-I-C-A-N."

"Daniel, just look them up the way I spell them. You already said the dictionary didn't have your words. Try mine, O.K.?"

"O.K., if you say so, but the teacher wrote *herican* on the board."

"Daniel!"

"O.K."

"Please, dad," Nancy said.

"Right. Now let's see how I can explain this to you. Let's say we were doing away with pennies, and from now on the smallest coin was a dime. Let's say you could turn in five or more pennies for a dime, and if you had less, then you had to just give them away. Now take the number 4,582 and let's say that 2 stands for pennies, the 8 for dimes. Tell me what the answer is if you round that number off to the nearest 10."

"Huh?"

"Ten."

"Ten what?"

Amy heard the word "ten." "Ten words I have to learn for spelling," she said.

"Later, Amy," I said. "Please. Just leave us alone until we get this straightened out for Nancy, O.K.?"

"O.K."

"I found the word," Daniel called. "It says, 'Violent wind and usually very heavy rain.' "

"Write it down, Daniel, and go on to the next word."

"O.K.," Daniel said.

"Now, Nancy," I continued, "this is really very simple. Whenever I say round the number to tens, you simply look at the number in the one's column. If it's five or over, then you cross it out and put a zero there and add one to the ten's column. Now, let's take the hundred's column; if I say round the number out to the nearest hundred, then that is your signal to look at the number in the ten's column. If it's five or more, you cross it out and write a zero in its place."

"Let's get this done," Nancy said. "Here are the problems. You give me the answers."

"I want you to understand this, Nancy. I'm not supposed to do your homework. You are supposed to do your homework. If you don't understand it, I'm glad to try to explain it, but it is your homework, not mine, and you are to do it. Understand?"

"No," she said. "I mean, yes. I mean, no, I don't understand how to do it; but, yes, I understand that it is my homework."

"Just so you understand. Now tell me, what is it that you don't understand?"

"All of it. I don't get it."

"Nancy, it is very simple. Just imagine . . ."

"Dad, I can't find *brese.*"

"That's *breeze,*" I called. "B-R-E-E-Z-E."

"But . . ."

"I don't care what your teacher wrote. It's *breeze.*"

"O.K."

"I've still got 10 spelling words."

"Later."

"I've got another paper to show you," David said.

"Let's see it," I said. "Oh, yes, a whole page of printed N's. How nice. Every one alike. Very nice."

I tried to give the paper back to David, but no such luck. "Sign it," he said.

I signed it.

"Aw, dad, I have to go to this Campfire fashion show at 7:00, and we haven't even started. Can't you help me?" Nancy pleaded.

"O.K., Nancy. Here we go. Now let's get down to some problems. Round to the nearest hundred the number 184,139."

"What's the answer, dad?" Nancy asked.

"184,100."

"What's the answer to the next one?"

"2,492,300."

"And the next?"

"Do it yourself. Nancy, this is your homework and you're supposed to be doing it. I don't mind trying to explain it, but it is yours to do. You do the next one."

"I can't."

"Why not?"

"I just don't get it."

"I found it," Daniel called. "Light wind."

"Write it down and go on to the next. No. Wait a minute . . . bring me your paper. What is that next word?"

"*Gussed.* G-U-S-S-E-D," he said.

"That couldn't be *gassed.* It doesn't fit. *Cussed, fuss, tused?* What kind of a wind is that? G-U-S-S-E-D?"

"How come you are listening to Daniel's spelling and not mine?" Amy asked.

"I'm not. Please, Amy, later. O.K.?"

"O.K."

"I know, Daniel, it's *gust,* G-U-S-T."

"That's what I said."

"G-U-S-T, Daniel. Look it up and write the meaning."

Nancy saw I was ready. "What is the answer to the next one?"

"6,431,000. We're rounding to thousands now."

"Next."

"536,000. Still thousands."

"And . . ."

"Four million, then seven million, then five million, and then we skip back to hundred thousands: 5,300,000, 67,900,000; see, we are rounding to hundred thousands."

"I see. You just listen to the number you are rounding to and then go back one number; and if its five or more, you cross everything out behind it and make the number next to it one more."

"Yep."

"And if it is less than five, then you just drop it."

"Yep."

"Thanks. We're done."

"Yep."

"I got it, dad," Daniel called. "Thanks."

"Yep."

"Thanks for signin' my papers," David said.

"Yep."

"Ten words," Amy siad, "Will you hear them now, dad?"

"Yep, Amy. Right now."

Those Phony Phoners
(and how to handle them)

Did this ever happen to you? You were deep in the enjoyment of a really good novel, and you were dragged away to answer a telephone call from a huckster who plucked your name and telephone number from a directory. Remember? The second you answered, he started reading you a prepared spiel that was carefully plotted to sell you insulation, storm windows or something you would certainly go out and buy if you really wanted it. It has happened many times, hasn't it?

And what did you do about it? Probably, you lied. You made up some flimsy excuse to cut off the conversation, but that telephone solicitor kept on talking, didn't he? Right? I know. Then what did you do? You made up another excuse; and, maybe then, you just hung up, feeling rude and uncomfortable.

The whole ordeal was rather upsetting, wasn't it? You thought about getting an unlisted telephone number. But you remembered how you felt about people with unlisted numbers, so you kept your name in the book. And the calls keep coming.

Soap. Magazines. Television repairmen. Photo studios. Every person in town seems to be pulling your name out of the book and calling you whenever you are otherwise occupied. That's how it is; and, believe me, I used to have the very same problem.

Then one night after three or four of these calls in a row, I remembered something my father told me many years ago. "The best defense is a good offense." It works too. Whenever you get the other fellow on the defensive, it diverts his mind from his own attack.

I thought of the whole problem in terms of war strategy. Those callers were my enemy. They were trying to rob me of my valuable time and infiltrate my lines of privacy. So I simply sat down and figured out a way to give the callers a run for their money.

I tried to reconstruct the callers' mode of operation. Callers make lots of calls every hour, and they read their spiel to as many prospective buyers as possible. Therefore, I figured, the greatest disservice I could provide would be to delay.

With my first caller, after war was declared, I simply answered, "Yes, this is he; just a minute." Then I went back to what I was doing. A few minutes later, I picked up the phone and said, "I'll be with you in a minute." Then back to my book. I had to remember to hang up the phone later that evening.

I quickly tired of that strategy, so for a little variety I developed a dialect technique. It involved using broken English. I waited until this fellow gave me about two minutes of his line, and then I said something like this, "Who you were calling? I'm no talk very goot." With a little practice I became proficient in German, Italian and Japanese accents. One bilingual salesman nearly caught me, but I switched into a singsong mumbo-jumbo, explaining, "I'm from Tunesia." When I grew tired of that routine, I just cut it off with, I'm no understand."

For weeks I added a touch of class to our residence by doing excellent impressions of an English butler or a French maid. And once I absorbed the spirit of the thing, I started working out variations. It got so that I was waiting by the phone, hoping for a victim to call.

Another technique is to launch a counterattack. When the pitchman starts, I repeat his name and go at him something like this, "Oh, you're Fred Johnson. I'm glad you called, Fred. I'm with the National Child's Book Foundation, and we've got a free set of books for you. What is your address, Fred? I'd like to come out to the house." With a counter-pitch like that, it's amazing how quickly they hang up.

Once, when a saleslady called, I employed the romantic approach. I told her she had a lovely voice and that I'd like to meet her right away. I told her to forget about the storm windows and insulation, that I'd take her away from all that. In a panic, she hung up!

If you're baby-sitting when a call comes, then do what I did. Let the caller talk to the little kids. It'll keep the kids amused while you rest up.

Now, about those characters who want you to answer a question for a prize. The prize is usually a free dancing lesson, and the question is usually something about whose face appears on the Lincoln penny. The last time I got a call like that, I said, "Just a minute. I'll go look." After about five minutes, I went back on the line and said, "Don't go away. I'm going nextdoor and ask my neighbor if he has one." When I returned five minutes later, my victim was still waiting, so I said, "Oh, the heck with it, I give up."

I really wanted to tell you about several other approaches I've developed, but the telephone is ringing, and I've been waiting for a call all week. Funny, since I started this counterattack, the calls seem to be dropping off.

Who knows, we just might bring back the door-to-door salesman.

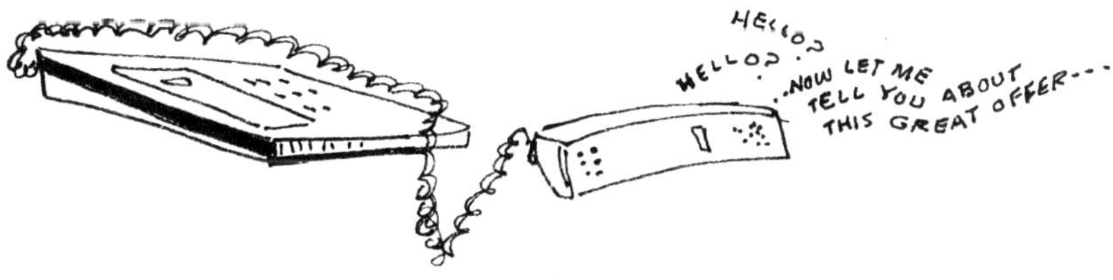

I've Bolted the Door on Togetherness

The one truly nice thing about taking your kids on vacation with you is coming home. Right now, I'm locked upstairs in my writing room in the attic; and I've made a deal with my four children that we won't say anything to one another for at least a full week. They are not to talk in my presence. If they run into any dire needs, they are to write it on a piece of paper and leave the message on my desk. I suppose in case of fire I'm doomed; but I'm willing to take my chances.

For six days, twenty-four hours each day, I have been totally exposed to my four children; and I seriously doubt that I will ever be the same. To say that I have kids coming out of my ears would be a gigantic understatement. Just the sight of my offspring causes violent indigestion. I ate in restaurants with my kids — every single meal. I slept with my kids. I shared every twitch and turn with them. We Disneylanded together, sharing the thrills and the rides. We flew side by side across America by jet, rode buses, taxis, boats, and streetcars. We shared tours, explored subways, climbed castle stairs and stood motionless together for photographs. We practiced "Togetherness" with a vengeance. In sunshine and rain, day and night we roamed the side streets of Los Angeles, and inhaled the smog. Yes, our eyes smarted together; and in the morning we choked together. We shared bedrooms, bathrooms, dressing rooms and closets.

We laughed. We cried. We talked intelligently and jokingly. And if just one of those kids even whispers at me in the next week, I just might become violent. I've had kids all the way up to my temples. I love my children dearly, but enough is enough. Take them, teachers. The summer vacation is over; and you are welcome to them for the next nine months. God help you.

Do I sound emotionally upset? Have I lost my cool? Well, you know how some children constantly interrupt and when you listen to them, they say, "Aaaaah," and can't remember what they had in mind? Not my kids. Not once did my kids say "aaaah." Instead, they said "gimme." Not in six days of constant interrupting did one of my children say "aaaah." Just "gimme." "Gimme a quarter. Gimme a dollar. Gimme a ticket for a ride. Gimme. Gimme. Gimme." And it was contagious. Bellboys and cabdrivers picked it right up. "Gimme $16.50" one cabdriver said to me. Imagine $16.50 for one cab ride with the kids. He had a strange system of charging for

each child, plus each bag, plus each mile, plus each minute, plus each question he answered, plus the fact that we took him beyond the city limits, plus the fact that he got terribly lost and had to double back a whole county. Why, $16.50 represents all the money I had spent on cab rides in my entire life up to that point.

A simple city bus ride in Los Angeles cost me $2.74 with my family. How they came up with $2.74 is beyond me; but that just happened to represent all of the money I had left in my pocket at the time. What a strange coincidence.

We've always made a point of allowing our children to be individuals. We try to allow them their little likes and dislikes without becoming violent. But eating out has become just too much to cope with. David likes hot dogs — and nothing else, except a little ketchup. Daniel is a spaghetti man. Nancy likes chewy things like sirloin steak. She will also eat Chinese food, provided that it is served by a gliding, kimona-clad Oriental. She doesn't like Chinese food; but she is crazy about gliding, kimona-clad Orientals. Amy likes fish and chips and candy bars. My wife Ruth will eat absolutely anything . . . that *she* cooks. Most other things are suspect. She truly believes that hot dogs are a plot to poison traveling Americans. The only thing that bothers me when we eat out is the size of the check.

Did you ever look for a Chinese restaurant — with gliding Orientals — that serves hot dogs, sirloin steak, spaghetti, fish and chips with candy bars, all at reasonable prices? Well, we walked around Los Angeles for hours; and when we finally found a restaurant that had the right variety, I didn't like the prices. Imagine paying 55 cents for a plain hot dog.

We ended up in one of those magnificent cafeterias where you get your choice of three entrees and all the trimmings that you can eat for a total price of 1.45 per person. Luckily, the entrees were spaghetti, sirloin steak and kraut with franks. They had fish and chips on another special.

It isn't that I didn't enjoy the trip at all. It's just that I didn't enjoy all of it. I kept saying to myself: "This vacation is for the kids." I must have said that a million times. Every time I spent another dollar, I repeated it.

And now that we are home, did the children enjoy it? Well . . . they haven't said. They haven't mentioned the fact that we even went. It is as if I drove them down to the Ritzee and bought them cokes and a side order of fries. The only difference is that when I do that, they usually say, "Thank you, dad." I guess they enjoyed it; they didn't cry or throw things at Ruth and me while we were on the trip. They all talked to us, at least to say "Gimme." But they did talk, and we feel that is something in this day and age.

Not that all of the money was wasted. We've got souvenirs — broken balloons, torn hats, stubs and more stubs. I've got a nasty-looking sore on my right heel; and my left little toe still hurts from the time I tripped in the dark while trying to get into the bathroom one night. My arm (as well as Ruth's) is extremely tender from being grabbed so often in a plea to buy something or other. Most of all, my emotional stability is shot. My eyes still haven't recovered from that smog. But, by gum, if anyone ever brings up the subject of Disneyland, I can throw out my chest and proudly report, "Oh, Disneyland. Last summer the wife and I took all of the kids on a jet and spent nearly a week in sunny California. Great! The kids loved it; and you know how we love the kids."

Maybe by then I'll be able to go downstairs and face those four wonderful kids again. Time heals all wounds.

Concentration

I think it is time that someone spoke up in favor of concentration. When I read a newspaper or a book, I concentrate on the thing I am reading. You might be able to get my attention when I am reading, and then again you just might not. My wife doesn't believe this. She thinks that when she says something, it sinks in immediately; and if she speaks it loud enough, there is absolutely no excuse for not hearing her.

My kids have adopted my wife's attitude, at least in regard to my hearing what they are saying. Someone is forever saying, "But I told you last night when you were reading."

Now, when I sit down to type out an article or a short story, people in our house hear the typing; and it always reminds them of something they want to tell me.

I don't know if you realize how a fiction writer's mind works, but I know how mine works. It works rapidly, once I get it started. I can visualize a story from start to finish in an instant. I can see the plot, and the troubles involving my characters; and I have difficulty pounding the keys fast enough to get the story down on paper before it gets away.

Usually, I get about as far as, "Charlie Fenner was in the worst mess of his entire career." Then my wife calls from the kitchen, "I heard from Jenny today, dear. Her daughter, Milly, has a little cold. George is drinking again. He dented the fender of their new car."

Can you imagine what this does to my train of thought? It is devastating. What does George's drinking and his fender have to do with my wonder character, Charlie Fenner, who is facing one of the worst messes of his entire career?

How do I handle this conversation from the kitchen? Well, I have what I call my instant rejector which makes such talk bounce right off my eardrums without registering. Then, later, when I'm finished with the short story and I'm ready to talk, what does the little woman do? She claims I ignored her. So I admit I didn't pay too close attention, and ask her what she wanted to tell me. But do you think she will? Not on your life. She gives me something like, "If you were too busy for me then, I'm too busy for you now."

At one time I believed that this was just something that happened only in our household. But I mentioned it to an attorney friend, and he said that his wife follows exactly the same pattern. He starts working on his closing speech to the jury, and this seems to be a signal for her to tell him the latest gossip. An insurance friend overheard our conversation and said that he thought we were talking about his wife.

I've researched this thing quite extensively, and the results are startling. Women seem to prefer talking to their husbands when they know they are too busy to listen.

They all use the same routine. They wait until you are using a buzz saw or pounding a typewriter or calling Berlin long distance to tell you about what happened to them that day. Then, when you stubbornly finish what you are doing and give them your full attention, they sulk and clam up. I wonder why?

I'd like to have a penny for every "Yes, dear" in response to a question that was completely ignored. I know I'm guilty. But I have the idea that women like you to say, "Yes, dear," no matter what they say; and I guess most men are guilty of this practice.

I suppose that at times the dialogue goes something like this:

She: "George, dear, little Danny just crashed your new car through the back wall of the garage."

He: "Yes, dear."

She: "I bought a new mink stole with those bonds you've been saving. It's O.K., isn't it dear?"

He: "Yes, dear."

She: "You are not listening to a thing I'm saying. Isn't that right, dear?"

He: "Yes, dear."

And so goes the war women wage against your power of concentration.

Know my solution? I bought a tape recorder; and anytime I'm working, I turn it on. It hasn't changed the situation very much. Whenever my wife hears the typewriter keys tapping, she still starts in with the chatter from the kitchen. But at least now when I'm done, I can play it back and find out what kind of trouble I've talked myself into this time.

Twelve Ways to Be Fat and Happy

You say you've got an inner tube around your middle, and you aren't even going swimming? People throw hints by yelling, "Hey Fatso!" when you walk by? The waitress at the corner lunchroom asks you if you'd like to try their Weight Watcher's Special "for a change"? Your doctor suggests that you drop a few pounds, "20 or 30" to be specific? You say you'd like to get on a regular exercise program, but simply cannot afford the time or energy involved? Let's face it. Exercising takes time — a good hour a day. And it uses up valuable energy, energy you could be using for more rewarding pursuits — like eating for instance.

Being in the same fat fix (people yell "Hey Fatso" at me, too), I feel well qualified to suggest a few simple ways to crowd in needed exercise without sacrificing that valuable time and energy that most exercise programs demand. I work on the principle that fatness is mostly a state of mind; and, therefore, the whole problem can be overcome with a few mental exercises. A few? Well . . . no. A dozen. But do these 12 exercises at least three times a day, and within a month I guarantee you will no longer be overweight. You will weigh the same; but your standards will be changed. You will simply reset your standards so that you qualify for an excellence award. I call it Fettig's "Don't Raise the Bridge, Lower the River Formula for Fatness." Sound simple? It is. Believe me! Now, let's get started.

First. Let us build a case for being overweight. What if we had a famine? Who would be the first people to die of starvation? That's right, skinny people. When you think of fatness, think of famine. Remember, you could live for a month off your fat. Isn't that a happy thought? Look at your fat as your personal survival kit.

Second. Remember, fat people weigh more. There is more of you to love; and so it follows that you are more lovable. Right? A man or woman who weighs 300 is twice as lovable as a slim person weighing only 150. Don't you want to be more lovable?

Third. Being fat can be means of self-protection. If somebody tries to rob you, you can sit on them. Carrying that extra weight around is like carrying a secret weapon.

Fourth. Having a large appetite is economical when you eat at a smorgasbord restaurant. You can eat $5 worth of food for $3, a $2 savings each and every time you eat out.

Fifth. Fat people get more material in their clothes, another savings that slim people are missing out on.

Sixth. Fat people get more breaths per day. Did you ever notice how a really fat guy breathes? Fast, like he's just finished a hard race. Air is free; and a fat guy who is panting breathes twice as much air as a slim Jim, another big plus for fatness.

Seventh. Fat people move more slowly and therefore get a better look at the world around them. Those nimble, wiry people are moving so fast they miss most of what is happening in the world.

Eighth. People remember fat people. Imagine a guy calling up and saying, "This is Average Arnold" or "Normal Nell." Nobody would remember them. They are the forgotten people. But call and say, "This is Fat Fred" or "Gigantic Georgia," and right away they know you.

Ninth. Really fat people can say things like, "You're not so fat, Charlie," and make others feel good. You have within your fatness the capacity to make slimmer fatties happier.

Tenth. Fat people are more buoyant. Did you ever see a hippopotamus drown?

Eleventh. People love to have fat people on their tug-of-war team at the company picnic.

Twelfth. Finally, and most importantly, fat people are jolly people. Everybody knows that fat people are jolly; and so, if you are fat, you might as well start being jolly. It is expected. A fat guy is jolly; and being jolly is fun. So if you want more fun in your life, stay fat.

Read these twelve mental exercises three times a day — maybe in the morning when you are hounding down your second breakfast, then at noon with your second piece of pie a la mode, and again in the afternoon when you stop by the bakery for a couple of those double-filled chocolate eclairs.

If you follow these mental exercises faithfully for 30 days, you just might grow to see a little humor in them.

The Borrowed Camera

"Honey," I said, "good old Jim down the street has solved our camera problems for our trip to the British Isles."

"You have a perfectly fine camera that takes beautiful pictures. Why don't you take that?" my wife asked.

"Mine is Japanese; and I understand that custom officials give you a hard time with foreign cameras. And, besides, mine takes 2¼ x 2¼ pictures; and I want to get the less expensive 35-millimeter slides."

"What if you lose it?" she asked.

"I won't lose it. Even if I do, he wouldn't mind. It's an old camera, pretty beat up. Even the winder gets stuck and the viewer is out of whack. But he showed me how to jiggle the winder and compensate for the crooked viewer, and it's O.K."

"I hope you know what you're doing," she said.

Unfortunately, I ignored her.

Two weeks later, we were in a London camera store trying to find someone who could jiggle the winder in the proper manner. No one could. Finally, a kind man took the whole thing apart and, after admitting that he didn't have the slightest idea of how to put it back together, put the parts in a little envelope and wished me the best of luck.

I took the remains to the London Kodak store and learned that their repairman was "on his holidays."

"Pleasant journey," they all called as I left their store.

I purchased another camera and went my merry way. I nearly forgot the incident until we got home and started unpacking. "Oh, here is Jim's camera, dear," I said to my wife. "Where are those parts?"

"Parts?" she asked. "I thought you put them with the camera."

"Oh, no," I said, "They were in with all that travel literature."

We went through reams of travel literature — but no parts. We went through six suitcases with a fine-tooth comb — and no parts. Somewhere between here and there, is an envelope full of parts; but in our house there are none.

I took the camera into the local camera shop. "What would it cost to fix this?" I asked.

"That old thing?" the dealer replied. "It would be a real waste of money."

"But I borrowed it and it broke, and I was just wondering."

He looked it up in the price catalog. "Eighteen dollars. It would be pure foolishness to fix it."

I took the camera back home. "Eighteen dollars to fix it, dear," I said. "What should I do?"

"You borrowed it," she reminded me.

"I know; but it was broken when I got it and . . ."

"You said it took good pictures for him."

"But $18," I said. "I could get a new one at the discount store for $18."

"You let that man take it apart," she reminded, "and you lost the parts."

I felt miserable. Then the mailman brought our slides. But I had miscalculated on the broken view and had a lot of nothing for pictures.

"Look at these slides," my wife said. "What's this?"

"That's Big Ben without the clock," I said.

"And this?" she asked.

"Trafalgar Square without Lord Nelson."

She looked at another slide and handed it to me, questioningly.

"An unusual shot of Picadilly Circus," I explained.

"It's unusual all right," she agreed.

"And that is Queen Victoria with her head cut off," I said.

"You cut the queen's head off with that camera?" she asked.

"It seemed like the thing to do. People were always cutting off heads in England."

"Not a picture in the bunch that is worth keeping," she cried. "What is this?"

"This is a unique shot of the Old Curiosity Shop that I took from that tour bus."

"It looks like the back of that charming bus-driver's head," she said.

"It is," I admitted. "You simply have to use a little imagination. You pretend that you are sitting in that bus-driver's seat and actually seeing all those places he was pointing out to us. I didn't see half of the sights he mentioned. I think he made up most of them."

"He was charming," she said.

"Charming! Just because he complimented you on your new hairdo. Couldn't you see through that? Really? He was just building up his tip potential. Gad! What a cornball, the way he sang *God Save the Queen* and *The Star Spangled Banner* at the end of the tour. Sure, he was charming; and that shot of the Old Curiosity Shop is unique."

"What are you going to do about the camera?" my wife asked me a few days later.

"I'll take care of it," I said.

Two weeks later she reminded me again.

Finally, in desperation, I grabbed the camera and headed for my friend Jim's house. I told him the entire story — the attempted repairs, the loss of the parts, the $18 estimate . . . everything. He laughed. "Forget about it," he said. "It was broken when I gave it to you. It just gave out. I'm sorry it didn't work out for you."

I made a faint offer to pay for a new one, even to repair it if he wanted. He brushed off my offers with a laugh. "Don't even give it a thought," he said. "It was an old, beat-up camera. I bought 20 years ago for less than 20 bucks. Forget it. Forget it."

He convinced me. We shook hands over the matter; and I believe we both felt good about the whole thing. Then I went home.

"What did you do about the camera?" my wife asked.

"I just told ol' Jim about the whole thing and offered to have it repaired or to buy him a new one; and he said to just forget it."

"Really?"

"Yes," I said. "It was already broken when he gave it to me. Repairs cost more than it is worth. I offered to buy him a new one and . . ."

"Oh," she said.

"Oh, what?" I asked.

"Oh, nothing," she said, "but you did borrow it."

Breakfast Out

"Mr. Fettig," the manager of the Village Inn Pancake House said solemnly, "your table for six is ready."

"Let's go, gang," I said. "They have our table."

"I want to sit next to dad," seven-year-old David said.

"Don't put me next to Daniel," Amy, age nine, said.

"I don't want to sit next to you either," Daniel replied.

"Quit arguing," Nancy, now 13, said. "We're in public. Try to act like human beings."

Ruth, my wife, smiled at Nancy. "That is asking an awful lot, Nancy," she said.

As we took our places in the attractive, comfortably padded, black leather booth, the waitress greeted us with a friendly smile and handed each of us a menu. It was like laying six live hand grenades on the table after recklessly removing the safety pins. Each of the children carefully studied the menu.

"What may we have?" Nancy asked.

"Anything you like," I said bravely. "Just make sure you eat everything you order."

"I'd like pigs in a blanket and an order of toast," Nancy decided.

"You can have toast at home," Ruth said. "In fact, you should have it for a snack when you get home from school instead of heating up those dollar pizzas."

"I didn't eat that pizza, Amy did," Nancy argued.

"What are pigs?" David asked.

"Dirty girls," Daniel explained.

"They are little sausages," Nancy replied. "They wrap these little sausages inside of rolled-up pancakes. They are real good, David."

"I want a Mickey Mouse pancake," David decided.

"They only serve those at Disneyland, David," I explained. "How would you like a nice stack of just plain pancakes?"

"I just want one big one, the size of the plate," he said. "And I want root beer to drink."

"You can't have pop," Ruth said. "Either milk or juice. Orange juice or grapefruit juice?"

"I'll take the orange juice," David said. "Large."

Amy studied the menu with great interest. "What is Suzette?" she asked.

"Where is it?" I asked her.

"Here," she pointed to the entry. "Three Rolled French Pancakes topped with strawberries and orange suzette."

"Orange sauce, I guess. Is that what you want?"

"No," she said matter-of-factly. "I just wondered. What are large German pancakes with apples and orange suzette?" she asked.

"Just what they say, I guess. Heavy pancakes with slices of apples and orange sauce. Is that your choice?"

"No," she said, "they just cost more than anything else. I wondered what made them so special. The Hawaiian looks good. Bits of pineapple with orange suzette topping. Whatever that orange suzette is, they sure like to spread it around."

"What will it be, Amy?" You've got to decide."

"I'll have half a grapefruit, large orange juice and pigs in a blanket."

"Amy," Ruth said, "you can't have both orange juice and half a grapefruit. You have to choose between the two."

"But dad said we could have what we wanted if we would eat it all," Amy explained.

"And that is exactly why you can choose just one. You couldn't possibly eat all of that. Now which will it be?"

"I'll take the orange juice," Amy said slowly.

"Daniel?" I asked.

"Pigs in a blanket and tea," he said with a decidedly British accent.

"No tea," Ruth said.

"But when we were in England you let me drink tea with every meal," he argued.

"We are not in England now. You may have either juice or milk."

"Orange juice," he decided reluctantly.

"What will you have, Ruth?" I asked.

"I'm trying to decide between the Blintz and the shredded coconut."

"Blintz?" I asked. "Sounds kosher. What is it?"

"Pancakes with creamed cheese blend, sour cream and tart cherries. I've decided," she said, "I'll have the shredded coconut."

The waitress came by, and we reeled off our orders to her.

"We don't have the shredded coconut today," she advised, and Ruth agreed to the Blintz. "It's so rich," she said, "but I love it."

I looked down at my waistline and went along with the pigs in a blanket.

When our food arrived, David asked Daniel to pass the syrup. Daniel had been waiting for this opportunity. "Which do you want?" he asked. "Boysenberry, apple, blackberry, coconut, raspberry, honey, or maple?"

"I'll take the regular," David said.

"This isn't gasoline you are ordering," Daniel said. "Which

flavor do you want?"

"He means maple, stupid," Nancy chimed in. "Don't get smart, Daniel, just because you are sitting near the syrup."

In a few moments all of the kids were digging in. Most of their plates held at least four varieties of syrup; and the only sound you could hear was the tinkling of forks and knives against the plates.

Suddenly the silence was broken by David's excited voice. "We forgot grace," he said. And without a second's hesitation, he blessed himself and the other children did the same. Ruth looked across the table at me and winked and I winked back; and we both joined the children as we thanked the Lord for sending this feast our way.

Later, as I paid the bill and the children walked out to the car, Ruth remained behind me. "Thanks, sweetie," she said to me. "I really enjoyed that."

"So did I," I agreed, "especially when the kids said grace. I guess we aren't complete failures as parents after all."

Go In for O'Blanskey at Left Aisle

While sitting there in church, minding my own business and waiting for Mass to begin, I felt a very distinct tap on the shoulder. "Mind helping us out this morning, fella?" a voice asked. "We're short of ushers."

I shrugged indifferently and finally stood up and walked to the back of the church. "There's nothing to being an usher," I thought naively. "All they ever do is give people a hard time and lead them down the wrong aisle."

Boy, did they snap my eyes open that morning! According to Webster, an usher is: 1) an official doorkeeper; 2) one whose duty it is to show people to their seats in a church, theater, etc.

But now that I've tried it, I realize that an usher is: 1) a keeper-outer of dogs, cats, mice and drunks; 2) a curer of hiccups, choking spells, crying, and mild fits of depression; 3) a fire-lane defender; 4) a move-over motivator; 5) a traffic director extra-ordinaire; 6) a misty-eyed collector; 7) an envelope pusher; 8) a dispute settler; 9) a dog catcher; 10) a car repairman; 11) a coat watcher; 12) a message passer; 13) a tract concealer; 14) a janitor.

The first thing the head usher asked me to do was to guard the right front door, because there was a dog trying to get in — also a drunk and a cat. "Birds," he explained, "are not a problem in our parish; but when I visited the island of Barbados, I learned that they have an usher assigned to the duty of shooting pigeons out of the loft before the people arrive. One Sunday, a pigeon failed to fall after being hit, and later, during the Mass, he came soaring down to the altar floor. 'It's the Holy Spirit!' one weak-sighted parishioner cried out." He smiled at this story and pointed to the door. "See if you can handle that cat and dog and drunk without shooting them, O.K.?"

After careful study of the problem, I persuaded the drunk to scare the cat and entice the dog to chase it. It worked beautifully. Next, I was told to stay near the back doorway in case we encountered any emergency medical problems. "We get at least one case of hiccups or a choker at every Mass. Just raise their arms or give them a good swallow of holy water. If that doesn't work, then slap them on the back and give them some gum to chew."

I explained that I had no gum. "No gum?" he asked. "What kind of an usher are you with no gum?"

"I'm just a fill-in," I explained.

The crowd started building up as the time for Mass neared; and people began standing in the rear of the church. I let them stay there; but "Old Watchful," as I soon began to call him, came charging over to me. "Want to have this place closed down as a fire trap?" he asked. "If the fire marshall saw this, he'd be up in arms. We have to keep these back aisles open at all times. Get in there and find room for these people."

"But it looks full down there," I explained.

"Don't let 'em fool you. There's plenty of room. Just get 'em to shove over. Put your hand on the pew as you face the rear of the church and hold up two fingers. Then smile. They'll get the idea."

"But what if there isn't any room?" I asked innocently.

"They'll move. They can pick up their kids and hold them, or crowd together by pulling in their elbows and arms. But smile at them; that's the secret. Smile and make them think that you believe in what you're doing."

I went down the aisle and, sure enough, some of the kids were taking up extra space; and a lot of the people had their arms spread out wide, making the pews look crowded. But when I tried that hand-on-the-pew and holding-up-the-fingers trick, it worked like magic.

As I walked back to the rear again, "Old Watchful" called me aside. "Some joker's got the parking lot tied up again. Get out there and see if you can move that Buick that is blocking things."

"But I don't have the keys," I explained.

"Keys?" he sighed, as if he really didn't believe in them. "Be resourceful, man," he said. "Jump the wire or push it. Pray a little, too, and innovate. That's the secret to ushering — innovation."

I went out there and tried to cross the ignition wires, just as the owner arrived. "Whatta ya doin', Buddy?" he asked. I tried to assume an air of authority; but when that didn't work, I reminded him that this was church property, and he wasn't talking much like a Christian.

Back in church, "Old Watchful" patted me on the back. "Do you know how to handle the collections?" he asked.

"Quickly?" I guessed.

"Yes, quickly, but with empathy," he explained. "You have to look like the church really needs the money. Think about how worn out that carpeting is in the middle aisle. Think about those Mass books and how badly they need replacing. Project; think poor — that's the secret."

With the way our food bills have been going up lately, thinking poor was easy. And it really worked; for as I started passing the basket, I noticed several men reaching into their wallets for more money than they had previously planned to give.

"Old Watchful" winked at me. "You're a born usher," he said. "Now pass out these mission envelopes."

When I finished that job, I walked to the rear vestibule, just in time to spot two teen-age boys squaring off against each other, fists clenched, teeth gritted, meanness sprouting out all over them. "What's up?" I asked. Both boys ignored me at first; but when I asked again, one explained that he was about to knock the other boy's teeth down his throat. It seems they had a mutual girl friend, and the sermon on loving all men just hadn't gotten through to them. I lectured them briefly on Christian conduct and made them go back into the church, each headed down a different aisle.

Now it was time for Communion. And just as I was about to walk to the front of the church to assist in directing the flow of people to the altar, a huge Irish Setter came bounding down the main aisle. "Old Watchful" spotted him about the same time I did, and we closed in on the dog together. I think it was the forward momentum of that large, unruly beast that made me topple over like that. I tried to maintain my decorum as I made a wild lunge for the mutt. But when I grabbed his rear legs, he nipped me. Caught by surprise, I'm afraid I didn't say, "Praised be Jesus Christ." Luckily, Father Riley (who is sort of a Francis of Assisi with animals) appeared on the scene. He just snapped his fingers, and when the dog ran to him, he simply patted him and easily guided him to the rear door. Certainly, if I were to ever usher in that church again, I'd bring along a bit of hamburger for such an emergency.

It was during Communion that the young boy started screaming. He had been playing with his model auto in the aisle and someone had stepped on it, knocking the front wheels off. He was making an awful racket. His parents were evidently up at Communion, so I took the young lad with his broken auto out into the vestibule. When I realized why he was screaming, I sat down with him on the floor, and we worked together on the car. Once I understood the workings, I snapped the wheels back in the proper slot. We were just completing the project when the lad's frightened parents came running back to where we sat. "We thought he'd been kidnapped," they frantically explained. I tried to tell them about his screaming, but they were screaming too loud to hear me. A small crowd soon gathered; and so I thought it best to get up off the floor.

"Watch my coat," a woman called to me as she darted for the door.

"The ladies' room is around the corner to the left," I called after her.

Just then another lady came rushing out. "Tell my husband George that I'll meet him in the car. I'm sick," she said. I nodded and then regretted it. Who was her husband George? There were hundreds of men inside.

As I waited for the woman to return for her coat, I spotted an odd-looking man dart in the back door and rush over to where the Weekly Newsnotes and a few other publications were stacked on a table. He placed a stack of papers on the table and rushed over to the tables at the side aisles and did the same. Then, looking both ways, he rushed out the door. I walked over to the table. Would you believe it? Tracts. Malicious anti-Catholic tracts. I gathered them from the tables and hid them in a dark corner.

"Old Watchful" rushed out to the vestibule just as the lady arrived to redeem her coat. "Thanks," she said, "I was in a hurry."

"What now?" I asked my leader.

"Pass out those Newsnotes," he said, "and, say, did that guy with those tracts sneak in here yet?"

I nodded. "They're over there in the corner."

"Good," he said.

We stood there in the middle of the onrushing tide, passing out the papers. When the last of the stragglers were gone I asked, "What now?"

"Clean up," he said. "You take that side; I'll take this one. Pick up the gum and candy wrappers, the purses and books and bubble gum and baby bottles, the gloves and hats and Yo-Yos and model cars and dolls and all of those other things that wonderful, civilized Christians leave behind in their mad rush for the door. And one more thing, O.K.?"

"Anything," I agreed, "what is it?"

He smiled a big friendly smile and patted me gently on the back. "Just promise me this, will you? Next time you see an usher doin' his job, don't think that he's some kind of a wise guy trying to order people around. Just remember, he's a miracle worker just trying his best to make things work around this church."

"But how did you know what I was thinking before?" I asked him.

He laughed. "I wasn't always an usher. I felt the same way before I got initiated," he explained. "Say, can we count on you again some time?"

I grinned. "Sure, but give me a little warning. I'll bring some gum and some hamburger and boxing gloves and a tool kit and . . . Aw, heck, call on me any time; I guess I could live dangerously one more time."

The Little White Bomb

I was ripe. Ready for plucking. My used-car buying time had come. I had the borrowed money in my wallet and I was ready to deal — cash on the barrelhead.

I was informed. I was aware that there were reputable and disreputable used-car dealers. I realized that when you paid too little for a used car, you were usually buying trouble. I'd learned that some lots recondition their cars and stand behind them after the sale.

Better than that, I had studied consumer reports, and I had a check list prepared by an expert on the buying of used cars. So prepared, I went forward to do battle.

The two main check points were these:

Have a body man look the car over to see if it has been in a wreck. I took it to body man before I bought. "What car hasn't been in a wreck these days?" he said. "Me, I'm in favor of wrecks. That is how I make my living, fixing them."

Have a good mechanic check the car out for you. I took it in and my "good mechanic" said this, "Don't expect me to look at that wreck. I wouldn't even change a spark plug in that model. It's a dog. All put together with sheet-metal screws. I won't touch it."

Exercising my constitutional rights, I bought it. I didn't buy from a used-car dealer. I let a dearler steer me to a private individual. "You can believe anything that fellow tells you," he said. Now, I didn't believe that dealer, just as a matter of principle; but I believed the fellow who was selling that little white bomb.

I don't recall what it was he said that accounted for the loud noise the motor was making — something about the cooling system and that the noise was perfectly natural and healthy. "Yes," he admitted, "the car has been in a little accident. Only about $600 body work. One of those slippery spots on the expressway. Only minor."

"No, she doesn't burn oil. Never had a bit of trouble with that car. My wife is quitting her job, and we just don't need two cars."

I made arrangements to give the car an acid test. On the way to school with my kids and their friends, I stopped off and let them all load into the car while I drove around the parking lot. "It is too small," daughter Nancy said. "We like Old Bessie" (my old car), daughter Amy complained. "Why get such a small car when we can't all fit?" son Daniel asked. "It smells," David concluded.

I was sold. The kids didn't like it; my mechanic wouldn't even let me drive it into his station; it had been in a major wreck; the price was too high. What more could I ask for? It seemed perfect. I made a firm offer. Then I unfirmed and compromised. I paid

$625.00 — cash on the barrelhead.

That little white bomb was mine, sink or swim.

At first, I wondered where all those gas fumes were coming from. I kept getting dizzy after driving just a couple of blocks. She was mine, all mine, and my other two cars sat blocking the driveway at home. I would now sell Old Bessie. Sure, she ran O.K. and I'd just spent $48 getting her in shape to sell and the kids loved her; but after all, she had 65,000 miles on her and she might have trouble soon.

I decided to take my new puchase out on the highway and check the gas mileage. I filled her up, and after only three miles, my gas tank was nearly empty. I got out, looked under the car, and found the cause of the trouble. Somehow, the gas tank had developed a hole. I was getting about three miles to the tankful. Old Bessie got 24 miles to the gallon.

I limped back to my friend the mechanic and pleaded with him to give my car a look. "Don't tell me you bought that dog," he said. "I told you I wouldn't work on it."

I plied him with a paperback copy of James Michener's *Hawaii,* and he let me pull onto the grease rack. He plugged the hole in the gas tank for $2.00, and I was on my way. I drove home and tried to forget about the tank of gas I had spilled on the city streets.

The next morning my little car wouldn't start. I tried everything I knew, which consisted of turning the ignition key on and swearing. After that, I pushed it out on the street and, against her wishes, my wife pushed me with Bessie. We didn't have any license plates for Bessie; but it would only take a push for a few feet (I thought), and then I was certain my little car would start. She pushed me for two miles. She tore up Bessie's grill pretty badly and didn't do my neck a bit of good.. Then we called road service.

"It's your automatic choke," the driver explained. "Better get it fixed." I recalled that Bessie had a manual choke.

I drove back to my Michener-reading mechanic and smiled a big friendly smile. "How is *Hawaii* coming?" I asked him.

He looked suspicious. "What is it now?" he asked.

"Automatic choke," I said.

"Why don't you sell that dog?" he asked.

"It's nothing much. Just a little grease or something on it. Adjust it or whatever. Nothing serious."

"Leave it," he said, "I'll work on it."

"Oh yes," I said, "this door hinge is acting up too. Will you squirt a little grease or something on it?"

"O.K.," he said.

"And I seem to be getting a little asphyxiated. Can you check for fumes?"

"Sure," he said. "And don't forget my advice. Get rid of this dog, quick."

His bill was reasonable. Just $8.00, and he fixed the automatic choke and the door hinge. But he added, "If that fume problem is what I think it is, then you need a head gasket, and I won't touch it. Take it to the dealer. He's equipped to do *major* work."

"A head gasket is *major* work?" I asked. "I thought it was a minor problem."

"With most cars maybe, but with this baby you have to pull the whole car apart. In fact, to do anything with this model, you start by removing all the sheet-metal screws. Everything is *major.*"

That head-gasket set cost a mere $6.11. Labor ran $45.50.

I pulled out of the dealer's garage, confident that I had licked the problems. From here on it was clear sailing. I was a good two blocks from the garage when the tweeting started. It kept getting worse, so I got out and lifted the hood (this was easy because the hood wouldn't stay closed anyway). It was something in the engine all right; beyond that I couldn't really analyze. I pulled into my driveway at home and looked under the car. There were two clamps hanging onto nothing in particular that hadn't been hooked up; and they were dangling along with my muffler.

Next morning, first thing, I took the car into the dealer. I showed him the muffler clamps that hadn't been properly attached and told him about the tweeting. He kept the car all day; and when I returned for it near evening, they hadn't started working on it. Finally, when I fumed and threatened, he had a mechanic(?) attach the muffler correctly and the bill came to only $2.38. That was 41¢ for a muffler strap and $1.95 labor. I paid it, although I didn't think I should. I got two blocks away this time and the tweet returned. I drove right back to the dealer and raved a little.

"Oh that," he said after listening, "that's your blower bearing. We can fix that tomorrow."

I left the car for two days, making certain that they had plenty of time to concentrate on the problem. When I returned, it was ready, and so was the bill for $21.16. This time $4.72 for parts and the rest for tender, loving, inspired labor.

I drove out of the garage, confident that the world was really a beautiful place after all. Certainly, my cares and troubles were all behind me. It was all downhill now. In fact, I was going downhill about four blocks from the garage when that bird sound returned. I wheeled around in a dangerous U-turn and sped full speed to the garage.

"I want to talk to your boss," I stormed. First, you sock me enough to overhaul this car. Then you charge me for parts you lost and labor for work you forgot to do. Next you come up with a phony story about repairing my blower bearing, and this car is still gushing fumes at me and deafening me with squeaks. I want a refund."

I never knew a manager could smile so confidently in the face of such wrath. That guy melted my heart of stone and then poured a can of *top* oil additive into my crankcase. "That should take care of it," he said. And then he gave me a refund of $18.20, the labor on the muffler and the labor on the blower bearing. I tried to get a refund on those parts, too, but he said, "Your car has new parts in it now." I argued that it didn't need those parts, but I was happy to get the $18.20.

I drove the car three miles on the expressway, and that little trouble light on the dashboard went on bright. This had to mean overheating or oil-pressure trouble. I drove the car back to my friend the mechanic, and he promised to give it a try. "I'm going to sell it," I promised, "But if it overheats in three miles and keeps squeaking, I don't think anyone will buy it."

"I'll try," he said, "if you promise that you'll sell it as soon as possible."

His bill was $5.00 for the first attempt, and she overheated in eight miles and started squeaking again. The next time he charged me $4.00 and said, "Sell it quick. The squeaking has stopped and I think I've licked that overheating problem."

I pulled the car into my driveway and decided to leave it there until it was sold. I was feeling high and low. Those gas fumes were making me high and my wallet was making me feel mighty low.

I put a coat of wax on the car and ran an ad in the newspaper. I used the key words "Sharp" and "Must Sell," and a half hour after the newspaper came out, a dealer was on my front steps. He offered my $500, and when he came up to $575, I signed the title. He'd taken that car out, run the motor, driven the car and given it a real going over, and he seemed quite happy with the results. The title was in both my wife's name and mine. The man made out a check in payment and gave it to me; and then we waited for my wife to return from shopping. We needed her signature on the title. I tried to entertain the fellow in the house, but he wanted to go outside and work on the car. I sat there sweating, expecting him to come charging at me with an end wrench, screaming, "This car is a dog and you are a cheat." Finally my wife returned home, signed the title and the man was on his way.

"Did you get his name, address and some kind of identification before he signed that check?" my wife asked.

"Yes," I lied; and beads of sweat broke out on my face. Stealing upstairs, I carefully read the signature on the check. I hadn't caught the man's name. Worse yet, I couldn't read his signature. I remembered something he had said about living down the highway a little ways, and so I made an excuse and left the house to look for my little white pile of trouble. Just minutes before I had never wanted to see that car again, and now I sought it desperately. I couldn't find it. Again I returned home and stared at the check. It was drawn on the account of a used-car lot, whose ad in the Yellow Pages gave the name of the lot owner. Finally, by careful handwriting analysis, I determined that my buyer and the car-lot owner were one and the same man.

The next morning, with heavy bags under my eyes, I was in the lobby when the bank opened its doors. The girl cashed the check without batting an eye; and as I looked at the 100-dollar bills in my shaking hand, I suddenly felt as if someone had just taken that little car off my hands. I'd been carrying the full weight of that car on my back for weeks.

Perhaps we'd licked whatever troubles that car had. That buyer might get 30,000 happy miles of driving without spending a cent; but I knew in my heart that if I had kept that little monster, it would have driven me to financial ruin.

That little white bomb had cost me $150 for three weeks of non-service. I looked fondly at Old Bessie and recalled that she hadn't cost me that much in the past three years. Gee, she looked nice all of a sudden. Nice and big and worthy. I climbed in on the well-worn seat and turned the key and the ignition. Nothing. I turned it again, and Bessie coughed weakly and went dead. I called the tow service, and the mechanic had her running in half an hour. "Your battery went down and that motor is soaked with condensation," he said. And sure enough, after we got her going and filled her up with gas, she stopped sputtering and her battery built right back up. By morning, I had the license plates back on Old Bessie; and the kids climbed into the back seat with plenty of room to spare.

I drove into my mechanic friend and gave him the good news. He smiled the most relieved smile I've ever seen come from a mechanic. "I'll keep that old one fixed for you at a discount rate," he said, "if you promise not to buy another dog like that last one."

I promised.

Family Treat - "All-American Eat Out"

"Children, daddy got an unexpected check in the mail today, and so, to celebrate I'm taking the whole family out to dinner."

With that simple announcement, total war erupted.

"I want a hot dog with just ketchup," David cried. David is seven and has developed a remarkable strong will in those few years.

"Let's go to Lucky Steer. It's real cool," Nancy, our 13-year-old pride, suggested.

"They don't have hot dogs," David said. "I want a hot dog with just ketchup."

"I want fish," Amy, age 10, said. "Across from Cut Rate Market they have the best fish and the best salad and the best french fries and . . ."

"I want a hot dog with just ketchup," David repeated.

"Why don't we just go to the Ritzee and eat hamburgers in the car? I'm so hungry I could eat three of them and a malt and fries," Daniel suggested. Daniel is 12 and can eat three of anything without stopping for air.

"Fish," Amy argued.

"Steak," Nancy said.

"A hot dog with just ketchup," David replied.

"Three hamburgers," Daniel demanded.

"Quiet!" I cried. "I don't know why we can't make this a pleasant, enjoyable event instead of a civil war. Now, I'm willing to go to any of those places; but what about your mother? Don't you think she should have something to say about this?"

"Yes," they all reluctantly agreed.

"O.K., then. We'll let her decide," I said.

"Mom," Nancy asked, "wouldn't you like to eat at Lucky Steer?"

"They don't have hot dogs, mom," David reminded. "And I want a hot dog with just mustard."

"Ketchup," Daniel corrected.

"Oh yeah," David said. "I forgot. I want a hog dog with just ketchup. The red stuff."

"How about a big pizza?" Ruth, my imaginative wife, suggested.

"Steak," Nancy said.

"Three hamburgers," Daniel added.

"Fish," Amy cried.

"A hot dog with just ketchup and maybe a little mustard," David said.

"NUTS!" I screamed. "I don't know why this family has to make a United Nations debate out of a simple question of where we eat. Why can't we work out a system so that we can avoid these silly arguments? Let's take a vote. No, we just did that. Get some paper. Each of you write down the place you want to eat; we'll draw one, and that will be that. Personally, I kind of like that smorgasbord that Roger has over on Columbia Avenue."

"Yech," Nancy said. "All that salad and garbage. It cost just as much as the steak at Lucky Steer, and it isn't half as nice."

"Nancy," I said, "I wish you wouldn't talk like that. It isn't ladylike. And Roger has delicious beef and chicken and . . ."

"Do they have hot dogs?" David asked.

"No," I admitted, "but sometimes they have Salisbury steak with gravy and . . ."

"Fish," Amy repeated.

"Steak," Nancy said.

"Three hamburgers," Daniel reminded.

"A hot dog with ketchup and mustard and maybe a little pickle," David added.

"I still think a pizza is a happy compromise," Ruth said.

"And I like the smorgasbord," I replied.

"Here's the pencil and paper," Nancy said. "I'll write them down."

"Let me write my own," Daniel demanded. "I want this drawing to be fair and square."

"Give me that paper, please. I'll write them down." I wrote down all six demands; and then before I put the pieces of paper in my hat, I made a final plea for family unity. "Whichever one I pick out is it. Final. No more bickering. No more discussion. We all agree to accept the winner and like it. No complaining about the food. We all go happily to the one that wins. Agreed?"

"I still think steak is a good idea," Nancy said.

"Fish," Amy said.

"A hot dog with the works," David added.

"I'm so hungry I could eat five hamburgers now," Daniel said.

"I'm not saying anything," Ruth said. "I think you are all being ridiculous. I don't care where we eat. I don't even care any more if we go out. They have the most delicious pizza over at the Pizza Hut, and you kids all love pizza. I just don't understand what all this discussion is about."

"I won't even draw a name," I said. "It is perfectly obvious that no one here is in a compromising mood. We'll just stay home. Any questions?"

"Why not give each one his own way?" Nancy asked. "All six

of those places are in the same area. You could drop each of us off where we want to eat and then go to Roger's yourself. Then, when you finish eating, you could just come by and pick us all up. I think it would be cool eating out alone for a change."

"Why not, dad?" Daniel asked.

"It would be fun," Amy added.

"Just so I get my hot dogs," David agreed.

"And I could eat a whole small pizza myself," Ruth said. "The kids always eat the pizza so fast that I hardly ever get any."

"And I could go back to that smorgasbord table as many times as I wanted without being razzed," I said. "O.K. We'll do it."

We all piled into the car, and I gave all of them enough money for their meals. After three trips back to Roger's Smorgasbord table, I had my fill; and as I drove down the street making the five pick-ups, each of my riders greeted me with a friendly smile and a thank you.

"That was just great," Daniel said. "I ate four hamburgers, and they were terrific."

"My salad was so good I ate it all," Amy announced. "And I ate all three pieces of fish, too."

"I see from your mouth that you had both mustard and ketchup on your hot dogs, David," I said.

"Thank you," Ruth said. "What a treat, eating a whole pizza."

"That was a cool idea," Nancy added. "We ought to all go out and eat together like this again, dad."

"Yes," I admitted, "it was rather nice for a change. Say, what about dessert? Any of you hungry enough for an ice cream cone?"

"Let's go over to Dairy Queen," Daniel suggested.

"No," Nancy said, "I'd prefer a snow cone."

"I want a fudgebar," David said.

"I want an ice cream sandwich from K-Mart," Amy countered.

"Hold it," I yelled. "Stop right there. You've all been individuals long enough. From now on your mother and I will make the decisions, and no more of this silly bickering. Right, dear?"

"Right," Ruth said. "Personally, I'd prefer getting a quart of lime sherbert."

"Yech," Nancy said.

The heated conversation continued.

"Dairy Queen." "Snow cone." "Fudgebar." "Ice cream sandwich."

"Nuts!" I bellowed, and silence reigned.

"A chocolate-coated cone with nuts." They all agreed and harmony prevailed.

How I Lost 20 Pounds in 10 Days

I was in the used-appliance department of the Salvation Army, when I discovered a good-looking bathroom scale. It was snowing outside, and I was well bundled up. I had on my heavy rubber boots, my overcoat and underneath it a full suit with long johns. I wore a muffler and gloves. I stepped onto the scale just to test it out, and my eyes bugged out as I saw the dial. It read 205 pounds. Now, I've noticed this little roll of fat appearing around my middle; and some of my friends have commented on the weight I've put on. But we don't have a bathroom scale; and I've just brushed these comments off as idle gossip. I didn't know how much I actually weighed; but I've held my weight at around 175 or 180 for some time.

"This scale doesn't weigh correctly," I told the saleslady.

"It's adjustable," she said. We both checked it, and it was set on zero. Then she climbed aboard. "It weighs me correctly," she said.

I got back on. It still read 205. "I'll buy it," I said.

I took the scale home and put it in the bathroom. Enroute home, I picked up a bottle of saccharin tablets. "Must be the sugar in my coffee that is adding all those pounds," I decided.

That evening and the next day I cut down on between-meal snacks and used the sugar substitute. When I weighed myself the following evening, I weighed in at 195 pounds. Just think of it. In just a little over 24 hours I had taken off 10 pounds. I had also taken off my hat, my muffler, my gloves, my overcoat and my heavy rubber boots.

The Following day I stayed away from all between-meal snacks and again used the sugar substitute. That evening, after I hung up my suit coat and tie, I weighed myself and had dropped another two pounds.

I was getting a mixed feeling as I passed by the candy machine at work — a feeling of pride and hunger. I held off weighing myself for two days; and this time I tried it without shoes and socks. I was down to 190 pounds.

I was also down to just my pants, underwear, shirt and slippers. I waited two full days for the next weigh-in. I stuck to my no-snack diet with no sugar and actually tried to cut down on the food I consumed at meals. I was cutting the size of my desserts in half. That night I took off my shirt and my pants which contained a heavy wallet, some change, a pocketknife, two address books, a fingernail file and a comb. I debated about taking off my long johns, but

decided to save them for a future weigh-in. I bounced gaily onto the scale; and there it was, right on the half button — 187½.

I talked with a few friends who had taken up weight losing; and they gave me a tip on the proper time for a weigh-in. "If you weigh yourself on the way into the bathroom in the morning, you are losing out. Wait until afterward. And don't drink any water when you brush your teeth," they advised.

Well, I did it their way the next morning; and I was down to 186. I tried the same thing the next morning, and even removed my long johns, but it stayed right there on 186. That morning I got a haircut. "Cut it short all over," I told the barber. He did, and when I weighed in the following morning, I was dressed in just my goose-pimpled skin. The scale read 185½. I felt that was inaccurate, since I was reading from a standing position; so I leaned over to see it more clearly. This being a rather awkward position, I merely placed my fingertips against the wall for balance. In doing so, I raised up slightly; and there it was, right on the button — 185. I'd lost 20 pounds in just 10 days.

It's funny, you know. I can't figure it out. I still have that little roll of fat around my middle. I'm going off this diet, though. It's dangerous to take off too much weight.

The Lector

Six times each year I mount the podium, look at the assembled parish, and in that short instant before I begin to speak, a sharp shiver runs up and down my spine, my knees grow weak, my eyes water, a drop of sweat forms on my upper lip. My throat grows dry and suddenly I discover I cannot breathe. Dead, unearthly silence fills the air; I move my lips and silently wonder if a sound will break forth. Fortunately, the sound comes, "A reading from the Letter of Paul to the Romans."

You pause. You look out on that sea of solemn faces and you feel worse. You still haven't managed to draw a breath successfully. You scan them all, trying to get friendly eye contact with your listeners. So stern they look. Even those you know warmly as friends seem to wear faces of stone. If only one of them would wink and break the tension, it would be such a comfort. "Brethren: It is now the hour for you to wake from sleep" (maybe that is the trouble, they aren't awake yet), "for our salvation is closer than when we first accepted the faith." You pause. (Always pause after a period. Look around; get eye contact, but keep your finger in place so you don't get lost and make a real mess of it.) You try once more to draw in a breath, but it sticks there on your lips. You read on. Carefully. Slowly. You speak each word with care; but it isn't easy without benefit of breath.

This isn't like the public speaking you learned in school; nor is it like addressing a convention or a group of business associates. This is more like *Judgement Day*. When you speak to a business group, you can break the ice by telling a little story to warm up the crowd and break down the barrier. But you can't insert yourself into this performance. You are here to read; and although you always believed that reading was the easiest form of public speaking, you now have to come to a different conclusion. You read on and try to put feeling into the words, to insert the meaning that is there into your delivery; but still you haven't successfully drawn a breath. Most jobs get easier after you do them a time or two, but this seems to be getting worse. Now you are nearing the end of the short Letter. "Let us live honorably as in daylight; not in carousing and drunkenness, not in sexual excess and lust . . ." (You wish you could at least smile at your audience; everyone tells you what a warm effective smile you have. But can you imagine smiling after a line like that?) So you conclude, ". . . not in quarreling and jealousy. Rather, put on the Lord Jesus Christ."

You stand there in shock. Someone behind you says, "Thanks be to God," and then suddenly you discover that you are breathing again. You are turning away from that sea of solemn faces and walking back to your kneeler. The tension starts leaving your body. You miss hearing the Gospel, but by the time the homily is half through you begin to hear again.

"I didn't do too badly," you tell yourself. "My voice was weak and shaky, but *they* wouldn't notice."

The Mass ends quickly, and then you are outside the church shaking hands with friends and looking for the wife and kids. "Beautiful job," someone says. "You didn't look a bit nervous."

"Nervous? What's to get nervous about? It's just reading the Lesson."

The Do-It-Yourself Auto Wash

"Kids!" I cried, "Nancy . . . Daniel . . . Amy . . . David . . . Hey, it's Saturday, and before we do another thing, we are going to clean that car of mine. It's positively filthy, and you and your friends who ride to school with you every morning are responsible. What say we all get out there and attack it all at once? Shouldn't take more than half an hour if we all pitch in."

Not a single reply. Just four cold, unmeaningful looks.

"Nancy," I asked, "how about you? Are you ready to help clean the car?"

Nancy compressed her 13 years of learning into deep thought and finally replied, "I have to go downtown to the bank this morning."

"The bank?" I asked. "What for?"

"I have to put some money into my savings account."

"Couldn't that wait?" I asked.

"They are only open in the morning, dad, and I have to get it in today. Money added to your account by the 10th draws interest from the 1st of the month. If I wait, I'll lose interest."

"How much are you putting in, Nancy?" I asked.

"Two dollars. Besides, when I add this two to the $73 I already have, it will make an even $75."

"Of course," I admitted. "Daniel? What about you?"

Twelve-year-old Daniel replied without a second's hesitation, "I've got a game, dad. I've got to hurry or I'll be late."

"Couldn't it wait?" I asked.

"No, dad. All the guys are waitin' for me. I've got the ball."

"And I've got the dirty car. Amy, you are the best 10-year-old helper around. Would you mind helping out for an hour or so?"

"I've got to clean my guinea pigs, dad. They smell. Mom says if I don't clean them right away, she'll make me get rid of them."

"The car smells too, Amy. I think somebody's salami sandwich is wedged down between the seats. David," I asked, "how about you?"

"Can I run the hose?" he asked.

"'Fraid not, Dave. You're just eight and you should be at least ten to run the hose. Remember last time how you got carried away and squirted the inside of the car because you forgot to close the window; then when I hollered at you, you accidentally squirted me?"

"But I've learned a lot since then, dad."

"So have I, David. Maybe I'd better do the car by myself."

"Oh, I'll help you, dad," David said. "Can I wash the motor? I like the way it sizzles when you squirt water on it."

"We don't wash motors, Dave. I told you that the last time I caught you doing it."

"I don't think you really want any help," David decided.

I resigned myself to my fate. I took a handful of rags and started for the driveway. Nancy came out and greeted me with her biggest smile. "Say, dad, before you get all wet and everything, would you mind running me downtown? I'm late."

"Are you going downtown?" Amy cried. "I need some wood chips for my guinea pigs' cage."

"Dear," Ruth, my wife, called, "if you are going downtown, there are a few things I need. Would you mind?"

"I'm not going anywhere," I shouted. I was somewhat startled by the loudness of my voice. More subdued, I continued, "I'm washing this car. It's so dirty that I'm ashamed to ride in it."

"Couldn't you do that later?" Ruth called out. "Nancy is late and we really do need these things now."

"Why don't you take your car, dear?" I suggested. "It's always nice and clean. It just sits there sparkling while mine works like a dog and smells like one too."

"What's wrong with the way dogs smell?" Ruth asked. "My little dog Jackie smells better than you do most of the time."

"That's because she doesn't have to ride in this car all of the time," I said. "I'm washing this car, and right now. If you are in a hurry, I suggest that you all come out and help me."

Still, no one volunteered.

"Amy," I called, "will you get me that big sponge?"

"Where is it?" she called from the basement.

"I don't know," I admitted, "just look around."

"Around where?" she asked.

"Never mind. I'll come down and look."

Finally, I found the sponge on the floor by the blackboard where one of the children had dropped it. I dashed up the steps, washed the car, and then pulled the seat cushions out. This revealed an old salami sandwich and an odd assortment of treasures, including two cards that had disappeared from my lone remaining deck, seven pencils, four ball-point pens, eleven different kinds of wrinkled trading stamps, three sheets of homework that the kids had sworn they had completed and lost, and one paperback novel. Besides, there were peanut shells, candy wrappers, chewed chewing gum, buttons, hair, and one dime, two nickels and three pennies.

I laid the entire collection on the picnic table.

"Kids," I cried, "come out here and claim your stuff. Take whatever is yours."

Daniel was the first to reach the table. "That money is mine," he cried. "I remember losing it. Exactly 23 cents."

"It's mine," Nancy called as she came bounding out the door. "The pencils, pens and money are mine. That is your sandwich, Daniel; I remember the day you lost it."

Amy heard the discussion and came upstairs and out to the table. "I lost those pencils and pens. I think the money is mine too," she said. "It was for candy, and I lost it."

David joined the crowd and he, too, thought the money and pencils were his. He didn't seem very determined about claiming the sandwich.

"I'll settle this right now," I said. "The money is mine. The pens and pencils are mine. Everything of any value is mine. I did the work and I claim the spoils."

"But, dad," Nancy said, "that 23 cents plus what I have in change would give me another half dollar in the bank drawing interest."

"It would buy half enough wood chips for my guinea pigs," Amy added.

"Twenty-three cents would buy a package of fishhooks," David advised.

"And I could get a hamburger and a small coke at Ritzee if I added just three cents to it," Daniel suggested.

"And any one of you could have had it, if you had only helped me clean the car," I said as I pocketed the money.

The following morning, the kids climbed into the car with their friends and we headed for school.

"It even smells clean," David said.

"Look at those windows shine," Nancy commented.

"I won't lose any more of my money in this car, that's for sure," Amy said sadly.

"And you didn't find any of my baseball cards?" Daniel asked. "Are you sure you checked everywhere, dad?"

"Not really sure, Dan," I admitted. "If you help next time, we won't miss anything."

"But this time," Daniel said, "I'd have missed my ball game."

"And I might have lost a whole month's interest at the bank," Nancy said.

"And I might have lost my guinea pigs," Amy added.

"Can I use the hose next time?" David asked.

I smiled. "Sure, David," I promised. "Next time we fumigate, you get to use the hose; and I'll wear my bathing suit just in case."

First Time Out. . .Almost

Boy, this'll really be a milestone in my life. My own son, Dan, making his basketball debut, and only 12 years old. This is gonna be great! I felt it in my bones. Sometimes I just sense these things, like I just knew Dan would grow tall and strong the minute I saw him in the hospital right after he was born. I said to myself, there's a born basketball player.

Ho! He missed his first two practice free throws. Darn basket in this gym must be a littler higher than regulation. A lot of the kids are missing, most of them in fact. I'm not prejudiced just because he's my kid. Not me. Ha! There. He made one. D'ja see that? Swish, right through. The kid before him hit the hoop with the ball, and it must have knocked it down just a fraction of an inch so it matched my Dan's aim. Oops! Dan missed completely on that one. Missed the hoop, the backboard, everything. Fingers must be getting sweaty.

There. Two in a row. Born athlete. (Bet I'd have been an all-American if they hadn't dropped me from the freshman team. I was too nervous — and afraid I'd show everybody up.)

Warm-up's over. "Who's gonna start? Why is Dan still sitting on the bench? Guess our coach wants him rested for when the going gets rough." Jump shot. (my Dan sure can jump, especially on those mornings when I'm trying to sleep.) Two to nothing — we're losing. Lucky shot. Foul. Missed. Ah! Our team's fighting back. Hey! We're ahead, 9-7.

My Dan's sitting right up next to the coach now. They're ahead. Now we're ahead — 10-9; 11-10; 12-11. Those kids are flying up and down court, panting and sweating, and there sits my Dan, the silent, inactive power of the team.

Half time. More practice shooting. Eagle-eye Dan. (Those kids on the other team must be terrified watching him warming up — realizing that Dan is waiting there in reserve.) The whistle. A pep talk and the teams take the floor.

Twelve kids on our team and the coach lets only seven of them warm up. One of them is my Dan. That means something, doesn't it? Sure it does. Maybe they could change the game so seven kids could play at once.

There's the whistle for the second half, and Dan has hit 15 out of 17 practice shots. The coach must have noticed it — Dan has a better seat on the bench. Here we go into the second half, and we're leading, 14-11.

Hard, fast playing, but no scoring. Time-out, and Dan's up there in the huddle. Gee, he looks anxious, eager, so willing. The huddle breaks up and Dan sits down. No sweat on Dan. Not a drop. He's fresh and ready. "Hey, coach, look at how fresh Dan looks. Those other kids look bushed."

Time-out. Another huddle. Dan is right there again. My heart is pounding like a triphammer. "Look. The coach has his arm around Dan in the huddle there." They break and Dan sits down. 15-14; 15-15. The crowd's screaming, cheering, roaring. The kids are anxious, and they foul and foul some more.

Not enough, though. If a couple of our guards would just foul out, then . . . but I wouldn't wish them any bad luck. We are still ahead, 17-15.

Time-out. Huddle. I'm getting mistyeyed from staring so hard. I don't even allow myself the luxury of blinking. Whistle. Dan is standing.

"Please, God, let the world see my son in action. Right now. Let him make his sports debut. We're ready, Lord. Let it happen." The whistle blows, and Dan sits back down.

Action! What action! A foul. Missed free throw. Rebound shot. Missed again. Jump ball. Action . . . swishing and swashing. Jumping. Missing. Sweating and missing some more. Precious moments racing by, and there sits my Dan. Another foul for us. How many fouls has that number 25 got now? Not enough. New score, 17-17. ZAP! 19-17. AAAH! 21-17 and 23-17.

"Hey, coach, what about my son, Sitting Daniel? Ya want him to get a complex or calluses on his rear end? How about it?"

Six-point lead. "Oops, one of our boys fouled out, and in goes . . . Where did *he* come from?" Another foul on us. "Keep fouling, guys. Maybe you can foul my Dan in." 23-17. Time-out.

Up jumps Dan. "Yeah, coach? Yeah, coach? Sit down? Sure, coach." Dan's looking sad and disappointed now. Reflecting my own feelings, and I guess the feelings of those five other benchriders and their dads.

"Sure, I understand, coach — either we win or they get another coach." Thirty seconds. "Come on, coach. We got a six-point lead. Call a time-out. Let those other five kids at least walk out on the floor. Hey, coach . . . can't you hear? Don't you care at all?"

There's the gun. The kids are jumping around, congratulating each other on a victory; and my Dan looks happy enough. (Now, what do I say to him in the car on the way home? I'd better not say anything.) Maybe next game he'll start. He'll start and he'll star, because I just know that kid is a born basketball player. Sometimes I just feel these things.

How to Attend an Auction and Still Stay Married

Every time I attend an auction, I witness a gigantic family fight in the making. It starts with curt little remarks like, "What in the world did you bid on that for?" The questioned husband or wife usually smiles a knowing smile and replies, "It's just perfect for the back corner of our garden," or, "I can turn it into a table."

If the unlucky partner is the successful bidder, then trouble really starts: "Now that you're stuck with it, aren't you proud of yourself?" or, "Well, you did it. Now don't expect any sympathy from me."

From the instant the auctioneer slams down the gavel until the hour of final departure from this glorious world, someone is going to hear about that unwise purchase.

Now, there are rare couples who see eye-to-eye on fix-up projects. But usually they are very young and just married; and everything seems possible to them. But for those old-timers at the game of fixing up, the basement or attic is full of clever ideas that just didn't work out; and so one of the parties is anti-everything in the game of product conversion.

Myself, I like to attend auctions alone. My conscience and memory of past failures take the place of my wife in this situation. I weaken and bid frequently for some outlandish product, but I ordinarily can limit myself to one bid. And in these days of plenty, there is usually one other dolt in the crowd who will outbid me. I have a conviction that almost anything is worth lugging home if it is cheap enough. Fortunately, for me, cheap enough is usually 25 cents; and the world is simply full of other people with the conviction that anything is worth lugging home if it costs just 50 cents.

If I had to place my finger on the one thing that has saved our marriage, I would have to say it is the existence of those 50-cent bidders who take me out of the bidding. Because if I bought everything I bid a quarter on, my wife would have either murdered or divorced me by now.

Recently, I attended an auction and limited myself to just four purchases: a huge steel planter on a stand, a toboggan, a ball of string about 14 miles long and a used record player. I must admit that this time I did not stick to my quarter limit; but these were items for which I had a definite use (or so I thought). Two dollars bought the 10-foot toboggan which was in new condition. Seventy-five cents paid for the huge bundle of string. The three-speed record player cost only 50 cents and the planter only a dollar. When I saw my wife's reaction to the planter, I left it right there in the field. For all I know, it is still standing there. My mathematics were as follows, "It is cheaper to lose the planter than the chief cook, bottle washer and love of my life." I shrugged at her reaction and lied, "I didn't really buy that. It was just there, so I sat my stuff on it."

Some people have especially strong feelings against certain items. I once bid a quarter on a huge moose head; and I thought we'd had it right there. While the auctioneer was looking for a 50-cent bidder, my wife was looking through the crowd for a good divorce lawyer. Finally, two ardent but unsuccessful hunters got the spirit and took the bid away from me. The bid was $3.50 by the time the one hunter successfully bagged the moose.

Another time, she bid on a cement mixer; and it was my turn to scan the audience for a lawyer. I could just see her cunning mind thinking how I would mix a couple of thousand yards of cement to install a new driveway. Somehow, though, my evil eye conveyed the message; and she stopped bidding at $2.00.

I've seen couples stand toe-to-toe at an auction, having it out right there, while the auctioneer waited for another bid.

Once, I saw a newlywed couple standing at different locations, each unknowingly bidding against the other in spirited conflict, because each wanted to surprise the other. The surprise came when they finally spotted one another and realized what they were doing.

If you ever examine an auction area after the crowd is gone, you will find several items left behind for the sake of marital bliss. The spirit of an auction can sometimes overcome the most prudent soul; but the thought of facing the family with your new acquisition is most sobering.

I've developed a sort of auction code that I try to follow; and I believe it might help others when attending auctions.

1. Don't bid on an item unless you can use it.

2. Look the items over before the auction, and set the top price you'd be willing to pay. Write down your top price and stick to it. An auctioneer is a top-rate, high-pressure salesman, and without a set limit you might pay an excessive price. If you can't look over an item before bidding, then don't bid.

3. Talk it over with your spouse before bidding. She might not agree with your idea; and it's best to know before hand. Decide which one of you will do the bidding.

4. If you have bought an item that bugs your mate, discard it immediately. Don't leave it sitting around the house causing conflict. It is better to take an immediate loss than to prolong the agony. If you discover the conflict while at the auction, look around for a

buyer. You might reduce your loss or possibly even make a quick profit.

5. Don't buy something that needs repairing unless you know how to fix it. Repairs are often so costly they make your purchase a bad one no matter how little you paid.

6. Unless you have unlimited storage space or an immediate buyer, don't buy items on speculation. Your friends will often say, "Why didn't you buy that for me?" However, if you do buy the item, you'll find that your friend didn't really want it to begin with. Let them attend their own auctions if they want items. You may think you know just what someone else wants, then sadly learn you were wrong.

7. If you can't control your bidding, stay away from auctions. Some people just can't resist an auctioneer's chant; and if you are one of them, then in the interest of economic stability, stay home.

8. Think about how you'll get an item home before you buy it. It is quite upsetting to find you've bought a piano and have no way to get it delivered. Many local dealers will move an article at a reasonable cost; but check it before you invest in a large item.

9. Watch the weather to protect what you buy. The sun might be shining when you buy that dining room suite, but dark clouds might be on the way. Bad weather usually means smaller crowds and lower prices, but once you buy something, arrange immediately to protect it in case of rain. Stuffed chairs can be ruined by a soaking; and many wood finishes are destroyed by rain.

10. Keep track of what you buy. Some people have a way of loading up their trucks or cars with other people's purchases. I find it best to load items into my car as soon as I buy them. But if this is impossible, then make a pile of the merchandise near where I am standing and keep and eye on it.

11. It is a good idea to study how each auctioneer works. Most auctioneers stick to the truth, but bend it a little. You have to listen closely to what they say, because many of them make general statements that mean nothing, using key words that mean a lot. For an example, one auctioneer I know likes to say things like, "That pitcher looks a lot like genuine cut glass." He didn't say it *was* "cut glass," but people hear the words "cut glass" and believe that is what they are bidding on. "I wouldn't be surprised if that was a genuine antique." Usually, too, they say the key word — cut glass, antique, genuine — a little louder. But if you listen to his entire spiel, you'll find that he is telling the truth. The trouble is that he is not really trying to communicate. He is trying to get the bid up with his clever words and yet stay within the law.

Generally, I stick to these rules, with the exception of my bad habit of making 25-cent bids just for fun. In the case of the bid I made on the planter that I left in the field, I had simply miscalculated my wife's tastes. She wasn't around when I bought the planter; and when I saw her reaction, I quickly unloaded the item.

I'm sure that if you attend many auctions, you will soon develop your own set of rules. Auctions are fun; and nowhere can you find such fabulous bargains. But look over what you bid on and determine its exact condition. Don't let the auctioneer make you bid more than you think the item is worth. Talk it over with your spouse and have a wonderful timc.

Auctions may have the makings of gigantic family fights, but what doesn't? For if you want to fight, you can fight about the weather. However, if you talk things over before you bid, auctions can be interesting, exciting adventures.

I'm Prejudiced About My Prejudices

The other day a friend of mine was explaining to me how free of prejudice he was. "Art," he said, "I wouldn't mind if a daughter of mine took a black hand in marriage. That's how I feel about it." I looked him square in the eye and reminded him, "Fred, you don't even have a daughter." He smiled and admitted, "No, I don't. But if I did have, I wouldn't mind." That's like the fellow who lives in a tent and doesn't mind who moves in next to him.

I'm prejudiced; are you? By prejudice I mean a judgment or opinion formed before the facts are known; a preconceived idea, favorable or, more usually, unfavorable. As I become more aware of the nature of my prejudices, I find myself more able to compensate for them and to act in a more Christlike manner.

How can we improve our attitude toward prejudice? By simply acting as Christ would act. This does not involve misquoting the Bible to show that certain races are inferior and therefore rightly put upon. It simply means accepting the fact that every person has a soul and is therefore equal in the eyes of God.

I have been guilty of many prejudices in the past. I have prejudged more people for more reasons than you might believe possible. Sometimes I catch myself saying, "They are all lazy, all on relief . . ." But I know that these generalizations are ridiculous. Negroes are as different from one another as people of any other race. They have their good and their bad. Some are beautiful; some are not.

Once, after reading an exposé on the Mafia, I decided that all Italians are members of the Mafia. Isn't that something? Do you know why we have the Mafia in America today? Because the Italians were smart enough to throw members of the Mafia in jail and make their lives unbearable in Italy. They ridded themselves of these undesirable characters. The Mafia is certainly not representative of the Italians in America. Such a tiny percentage of the American-Italian people are connected with the Mafia that it wouldn't represent one percentage point.

What about prejudice against the Polish people? Some people may be motivated by prejudice when they tell Polish jokes, but most of us see the humor of the stories and realize that basically they are the same as those told about the Irish, the English, the Scotch, the French, the Germans, the Scandinavians and the Negroes through the centuries.

I have prejudices about women. I resent it when they have a

better education than I, and especially when I learn that a woman makes more money than I do. Whenever I hear a woman speaking out with authority, my male chauvinism comes to the fore. I simply cannot listen to Dr. Joyce Brothers on the radio without making derogatory remarks.

I have a special prejudice against workers who are paid premium rates for overtime, especially when I am paying for the work. Not once in my lifetime have I worked at a job that paid a premium for overtime; so when I hear of a worker getting double time or triple time on holidays, it bugs me.

I resent certain clergy, lawyers, doctors, insurance salesmen, door-to-door salesmen, telephone solicitors and custom officials. Most custom officials get my dander up.

If I were to put my finger on the most important thing that has made communicating difficult for me, I would have to admit that it is my prejudices. Most of my prejudgments are incorrect. If I could walk into a situation or up to an individual and, with no self-made hang-ups, dive in and discuss a problem with an open mind, I would have an excellent chance of getting good results. But this would be perfection. The simple truth is that we all have hang-ups, memories, false ideas, preconceived ideas and opinions that simply are not true.

I was taught that the Japanese are a very untrustworthy race. "Remember Pearl Harbor," I was told. Since then, I spent a year in Japan and concluded that the Japanese are a most trustworthy group of people.

Once, in Japan, a fellow GI from the deep, deep South came in late at night extremely intoxicated. He spotted me sleeping on my cot, climbed on top of me and started choking me. I was half awake when I spotted the wild look in his eye and heard him screaming, "You rotten Yankee, you killed my great granddaddy." Until that night, I never had a bit of prejudice against Southerners. Now, I'm not so sure.

Having accepted the fact that I am now middle aged, I find I have prejudices against young people and old people. Maybe that is the key to the whole difficulty. We tend to be prejudiced against those not in our age bracket.

At one time in my life, I smoked and drank to excess. Now, I have prejudices against people who smoke and drink. Those who act or react differently than we do are prime targets for prejudice.

After 20 years of experience in handling personal-injury claims, I've learned that most people, regardless of race or nationality, are basically honest. But if you show that you are prejudiced, they try to compensate for your attitude; and then it is easy for you to take their indifference as proof that your prejudgment was correct. After many errors in this area, I extended the saying, "You are what you believe you are," to, "People react the way you expect them to react." Then I realized that if I could simply convince myself that a man would treat me honestly, then my attitude would show itself when I met the man and he would act accordingly. What I was really doing was using prejudice in reverse. I approached each claimant with the attitude that I fully expected him to be perfectly honest. Sometimes all of my senses warned me that I was dealing with a dishonest person. Nevertheless, I would plod ahead, letting him know that I planned to act in an honest manner and expected him to do the same.

When events proved that the claimant was not walking the straight and narrow, I would immediately call the failure to the man's attention. I'd do it in a straightforward manner. If it was an obvious attempt to defraud, I'd say, "I know that it is tempting to try to make the most out of this situation, but let's both be honest, O.K.? We'll both feel a lot better when we get done if we try to be honest all the way."

Since I discovered the secret of using prejudice in reverse, I have found that my job is 10 times easier. I feel better about everthing I do and have noticed that others greatly appreciate my new attitude.

It's easy to say that we have no prejudices; but in the face of real issues our innermost feelings often betray us.

I'm growing. I've got as far to go as anyone in order to look at my fellow-man in a Christlike manner, but I'm working on it. I'm admitting my hang-ups and working on them every day. Tomorrow, I hope to be a little bit less unfair than I am today.

An Anniversary Is What It Was

"Ruth, darling," I called down the basement stairs, "I love you."

"No," she replied.

"Please, sweetheart. I love you madly."

"Don't *madly* me" she snapped. "The answer is no."

"But remember your promise — for better, for worse, for richer, for poorer, in sickness and health 'til death do us part."

"So drop dead, lover boy."

"But I'm mad about you — positively insane about you. How could you ever think that blonde in my office could mean a thing? Come on, sweetie," I pleaded, "it's our 15th wedding anniversary, and we simply must go out and celebrate it."

"I'm doing the wash. I'm the family slave. I cook and sew and work from sunup until sundown while you flirt with the girls at work."

"You're going to feel like crawling under the carpet when you find out what that blonde was doing in my office."

"If I do, I'm sure to meet you there, you worm."

"She was a salesgirl," I explained.

"And I can just guess what she was selling," she said sarcastically.

"She was a salesgirl from Modern Furrier."

"Did she want your pelt, you skunk?"

"She was delivering your anniversary present."

"Honey," she purred as she crept up the stairs, "do you mean . . .?"

"Don't *honey* me," I said. "After your remarks in my office when you walked in and saw her there, I told her to take it back."

"You what?"

"I told her that I had changed my mind and that I didn't want the coat."

"Then it was a coat? What kind did you buy me, you sweet lovable brute?"

"Don't come near me," I cried. "After all you said, I didn't buy you any kind."

"Mink?"

"Skunk. That's what you just called me."

She came closer and closer, eyes aglow. "Where is it, tiger? Let me see it."

"It's in the store, on the shelf, ready for resale by now. What kind of fool would give a jealous wife a mink stole just for a lousy 15th wedding anniversary that she doesn't even want to go out and celebrate?"

"Let me just wrap it around me and find my way to heaven," she sighed.

"Back to your work area, slave."

"I'll be ready to go in just 10 minutes. Right on time, you wonderful hunk of man," she whispered in my ear.

"I think we should just sit at home and fight instead."

Incredibly, 10 minutes later she was downstairs, dressed, and ready to go.

"How did you get ready in 10 minutes? During our 15 years of marriage, you have never made it in less than two hours."

"I'll just stand here and close my eyes; and you can slip up and put it over my shoulders."

"What'll it be tonight? Hamburgers or hot dogs?"

"We'll have champagne and candlelight, and I'll wear my mink all through dinner like some of the ladies do."

"'I think I prefer hamburgers."

"I'm closing my eyes, dear. They've been closed for some time now. Sock the mink to me, darling."

"I've decided," I said. "Hamburgers it will be. We'll go over to the Ritzee, and we can eat in the car."

Quietly, I tiptoed into the closet and took that beautiful stole from the box. I felt 20 feet high, and actually bumped my head as I walked out of the closet. It wasn't really good enough, not the very best they had. But in mink, the very best cost more than the house we live in.

She cried when I slipped it on her shoulders and said that she was the happiest woman in the world.

The kids came downstairs and found us there kissing and hugging; and sure enough, we were an hour late for our reservation at the restaurant, just like always.

The music was soft, the light low; and we talked about kids and dogs and houses, and 15 glorious years that had somehow slipped by without any critical concussions. Then we thanked God for sending us together.

The Family That Prays Together . . .

"Family, I gathered you together here this evening to discuss a very important subject — praying together at Mass. Week after week, we each pay our respects to the Lord; but recently I've noticed a certain falling out. Like last Sunday, Nancy, you went to the 9 o'clock Mass when Daniel and I went to the early 5:45. David, you had me drive you to and from the 11 o'clock Mass; and your mother went to the 12:30. Amy, you finally went to the 5 o'clock evening Mass on your bicycle. Now, tomorrow is Sunday again; and I propose that we all go together in one car as a family unit. How about it gang?"

Nancy began the melee. She is fresh out of the eighth grade and likes new clothes for special occasions; to her, just getting out of bed in the morning is a special occasion. She baby-sits and is financially semi-independent. "I want to go to the 9 o'clock Mass and sit with my friends," she said.

Daniel, our towering 13-year-old son, got that sadistic gleam in his eye. "Let's go to the 5:45 Mass, dad; I like to get an early start."

"Dan," I reminded, "last Sunday you went right back to bed after we came back from the early Mass. From now on, the 5:45 is definitely out, unless I have to serve as lector." I turned to my wife, "How about it, honey, what time do you like?"

She smiled and said honestly, "You know I can't stand daylight. I'm a night person. Why don't they have a midnight Mass all year round, not just at Christmas?"

"Sorry, dear, we have to work within the existing conditions. Now, when would you prefer?"

"How about 11?" she said. "That's not too early and not too late."

Eleven-year old Amy scowled. "Don't do that, Amy," I said "Don't you want to grow up to be beautiful? Smile. It takes just about five muscles to smile and nearly thirty-seven muscles to scowl."

Amy shrugged. "So I become muscle-bound. So who cares? At 11 o'clock, Father talks for an hour about nothing. He goes on and on."

"Shame on you, Amy," I said. "You mustn't criticize that nice old man, especially since he is a priest. How about the 9 or the 12:30? David, which do you prefer?"

"I want to go fishin'," David said. David is nine and, as yet, has not had a stirring religious encounter.

"David, you must go to church on Sunday. It's the one day set aside for the Lord."

"The fish bite better on Sunday," David said. "I always catch more fish on Sunday."

"Probably because you always go to church on Sunday before you fish."

Ruth decided we had floundered long enough under my dynamic leadership. "We'll go to the 9, dear, if it's all right with you," she said.

"Nine it is," I consented. "We'll all walk down the aisle together at five minutes to nine. Is it agreed?"

"Why can't I sit with my friends?" Nancy asked.

"Aren't we your friends, Nancy?" I inquired.

"Not like my friends are my friends. I'm embarrassed to sit next to Daniel and Amy, the way they act. Daniel sings loud and off-key like some kind of a monstrosity; and Amy always slouches down in the seat like she's drugged."

"Nancy, these are your sister and brother. They might find slight imperfections in you, too; but we must learn to live together in harmony. Amy, you sit up straight tomorrow; and, Daniel, you sing softly. I was wondering what that ungodly sound was that I heard at Mass last Sunday. Sing quietly or else not at all."

Daniel looked over at Nancy. "You're not such a hot singer, Nancy. Not so hot at all . . . I wouldn't complain about anybody's singing and . . ."

Nancy looked right back. "I didn't say I was so hot . . . I just said that you were lousy."

Amy decided she had remained silent long enough. "You're not so smart, Nancy. You slouch over in church, too. You're not so perfect . . . you think you're smart because you are going to high school; and you think you're too good to sit with the rest of us."

Nancy heard part of what Amy was saying, even though she was still educating Daniel. "I didn't say I was too good, Amy. I just said that it was embarrassing the way you all act."

"Children!" I yelled, "we are all going to the 9; and we are all going to walk down the aisle together; and we will all sing softly and sit up straight and conduct ourselves in an orderly Christian manner."

David's eyes lit up. "Since we are going together, dad, will we eat at the Pancake House after?" he asked.

There was a sudden silence after that question; and I felt 10 eager eyes glued on me, waiting for an answer. "Now, what brought that up?" I asked weakly.

Nancy reached across the table and actually touched my hand. "The last time we all went to church together, you took us out to breakfast," she said politely. "How about it, dad?"

Ruth didn't say anything. She didn't have to. The fact that she wasn't saying anything like, "I'll fix us a nice breakfast after Mass," or, "That's too expensive," was a pretty good clue that she also welcomed the idea of eating out for breakfast. I did the only thing I could do, under the circumstances. I smiled weakly and looked at David. "Why, that is a good idea, David. A great idea! The family that prays together eats out together."

It was a wonderful experience. Amy sat up straight. David forgot about fish for a few hours and concentrated on praying and eating pancakes with sausage. Daniel sang badly but softly; and Nancy sat with us. Of course, she steered us as we entered the church so that we just happened to sit right next to her girl friends. Ruth looked beautiful even though she is a night person; and I could tell that she shared the same wonderful feeling that I experienced when we walked up to Communion together as a family unit.

It was just before I went to pay the check at the restaurant that Daniel spoke up. "How about next week, dad? Remember, the family that prays together eats out together."

"Next week?" I asked weakly. "Next week? Well, next week I'm sure that Nancy will want to go to church with her girl friends; and Amy will want to ride her bicycle to the 5 o'clock; and maybe we can arrange for a special midnight Mass for mom. David will have to get to Mass so it won't interfere with his fishing; and I'm going to make sure I have a big breakfast at home before I go. Why don't you go with me, Dan, after we eat at home?"

"I get the message, dad," he said. "What you really mean is that too much praying together isn't really good for a family, especially when the family that prays together eats out together."

"You got it, Dan. You know, you're getting smarter every day. Taller and smarter and better looking."

"Yeah," Nancy added, "now if you can just teach him not to sing at all in church, I'll sit next to him again."

Soaring

Last week a small carnival came to one of our local shopping centers. It consisted of just a half-dozen rides and three or four games of chance. Daniel, my 13-year-old son, was shopping with me; and although the rides weren't enticing enough to lure Daniel's hard-earned money out of his pocket, nevertheless they were interesting enough to warrant spending a little of dad's money. I bought him a dollar's worth of tickets, and he happily ran off to use them.

He was riding on something they called the "Sky Ride" when I spotted him. He wore a smile a foot wide; and when the sun caught the metal braces on his teeth, they glistened. Daniel was sitting in the seat with his arms hanging loosely from his beanpole frame. Daniel, whose shoe size changes every two weeks. Daniel, who seems to grow another two inches every time I look at him, and who at times seems so uncoordinated that you'd swear he couldn't chew gum and walk at the same time. (He'd better not chew gum, not after what those braces cost me!)

As the ride raced around, the wind caught his hair and blew it out of his eyes. He couldn't know that, while watching him, I was filled with a great deal of pride. Pride, yes, and envy, too. For at that moment Daniel didn't have a single care in the world. He was just a happy, happy kid who had the ability to enjoy what he was doing to the fullest degree. His body hung limp so that the full sensation of soaring could soak through his being. There wasn't an ounce of hostility in his apperance — not a speck of frustration or responsibility or worry. Every time that ride came back down near the ground, Daniel's long, dangling legs would come within a foot or so of touching the ground. Then he would soar up, up and away — as Superman would do without benefit of that seat and that framework and that roaring diesel engine that propelled the contraption.

And there was nothing to worry about at school, because somehow, just barely, Daniel had passed the eighth grade. Of course, in a few months he would be facing a new life in high school. But these and the world problems reported each evening in the newspaper and on television were far from him at this moment.

Daniel was feeling great, and growing and soaring up and down like nobody else, because the crowd was very small that early in the day; and no one else cared to soar like him. As the ride went around and up and down, my own life rushed before me. I recalled all of the heartaches I'd faced in high school and in life ever since that wonderful summer between eighth grade and high school; and I knew that, for Daniel, life would never again be as carefree and wonderful as it was for him here and now. When the ride stopped, Daniel walked over to me and asked, "O.K. if I go on that ride once more, dad?" And I almost shouted my reply, "Yes, Daniel, yes. And enjoy, enjoy. Savor it, if you can. And try to hold that smile that you are now wearing. Try not to let the world get to you, Dan."

"Huh?" he asked.

And I told him, "Never mind. Just get back on that ride and soar some more."

Daniel soared for a whole dollar's worth more, because I wanted him to get all of the carefree, innocent enjoyment he possibly could. Later, I tried it myself, but I took with me all the cares that we so-called "grownups" acquire through the years, and when that noisy contraption soared, my stomach flipped, and I couldn't get back on the ground fast enough for comfort.

Since then, I've been studying Daniel: as he splashed gracefully into the water at the lake; when he arched that basketball right through our neighbor's hoop; when he tossed that heavy bagful of Sunday newspapers over his shoulder to go on deliveries. And darned if he didn't still have that same innocent, fascinating smile, braces and all. I felt warm and proud inside that this was my son, our boy. I close my eyes and pray, trying to forget the newspaper headlines about drugs and wars and riots and asking God to keep him always as happy and uninhibited and honest as he is today.

So Much in a Touch

As I sat in church this morning, an usher walked by holding the collection basket and touched me as he passed. He gently squeezed my shoulder as a sign of friendship and fellowship; and although I exchanged greetings with a dozen other individuals and immediately forgot them, I still remember Frank's greeting, simply because he touched me.

At an open meeting of Alcoholics Anonymous which I attended recently, I listened to an attractive middle-aged lady who was the guest speaker. She told the audience about her own battle with the bottle. She's tried AA perhaps a dozen times; and each time she'd failed. She fell back into her hopeless drinking pattern. "Then one evening," she said, "I attended a meeting where the speaker was talking about his own failures and his final acceptance of the program. I was sitting in the front row. The man told how he believed that the fellowship of AA was the real secret of his sobriety. Then he stepped down from the lecture platform and reached out and put his one hand on my shoulder and his other hand in mine. And touching me, he said, 'The miracle of AA is that we are together, you and I, and together we can face this world without alcohol.' "

"I haven't had a drink since then," she explained. "His touch was like a miracle to me. I was no longer alone with my problem. I had another human being who cared about me and understood my problem. From that moment on, I accepted AA and began a happy new way of living."

In time of trouble, a gentle, understanding touch can mean more than all the words of consolation in the world.

In a world where everything comes sterilized in neat plastic wrappers, we sometimes lose our wisdom and understanding. We get away from meaningful things and toss them off as sentimentalism. We deepfreeze our emotions and substitute glibness. As we replace the real things with the slick, we diminish our joys in life and deepen our anxieties.

The late President John Fitzgerald Kennedy understood the power of touch. Shortly before he was killed, he walked to the waiting crowds in Texas and shook every hand he could reach. He touched the people, and they were deeply touched by it.

You can increase your personal warmth and your power to love and be loved by your fellow-man simply by inserting a genuine feeling into your handshake. Shake hands with your fellow-man. Look him in the eye. Pat him on the shoulder. Add sincerity to your conversation. Don't just utter meaningless expressions. Say

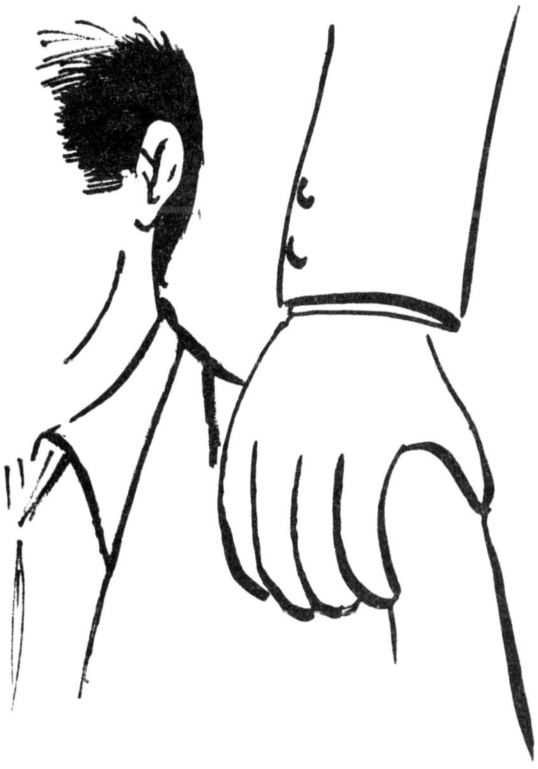

something and mean it. It is so easy to get into the rut of living a life of mediocrity. The next time you meet a friend, shake his hand. Tell him you are honestly glad to see him again. This isn't a time-consuming thing. You are probably already spending the same amount of time in unmeaningful chatter. Put your whole self into your conversations and greetings, and suddenly, all life will take on a new meaning, a new zest, for you. Your mediocre friends will suddenly become exciting, interesting people, because they will reflect your own spirit of full living.

With your touch of fellowship, your friendships will deepen into more meaningful relationships. You will somehow dissolve that quick, slick modernness that takes the meaning out of life.

So, try touching people. It will get easier as you go along. If you will touch people on the hands and arms and shoulders, soon you will touch them in their hearts and souls. And the world will gradually become a more beautiful place in which to live.

Get Your Jollies at the Follies

Every community, whether culturally or sadistically inclined, should have at least one high-spirited amateur follies production each year. Like a bad flood or a devastating tornado, working on a follies makes lifelong comrades out of the survivors.

To begin with, every follies needs a cause, a reason, a heaven that looks almost worth all that hell — something that the community cannot do without, some item that can be bought with the profit. Our cause was a cardiac-arrest cart for a local hospital. Now, there is something around which you can rally a ticket-selling campaign. If you have a heart attack, this cart might save your life . . . keep you alive longer . . . save the lives of your loved ones, and maybe even the life of your breadwinner.

Eureka! Not only did our cause inspire the ticket-buying public, but it also inspired our cast. We were no longer mere amateur talent displaying our worst and our best for the good old cause, but miniature Doctor Schweitzers and Florence Nightingales stumbling around onstage benefiting all mankind.

The professional way to approach an ordeal like this, I am told, is to call on professionals. The fact that they charge outrageous prices will be quickly overlooked if the venture is a success. However, it just might send you to the grave if the venture is a failure and you were lucky enough to be on the original committee which proposed the whole disaster in the beginning. Fortunately, we succeeded; and so the formulating committee is now looked upon as a group of far-sighted crusaders. Financially, the venture was a success. But let me tell you, now, about things less important than money — things like sanity, vanity and calamity.

The ordeal began on a merry note. The truth is that everyone was gassed at the start. The wives used their womanly wiles on their husbands. That is, they said threatening things like, "If you want me to love you, darling, you'd better come with me to this meeting." Wise husbands capitulated. Most wives followed preplanned instructions and comforted their unwary husbands with words like, "All you have to do, dear, is help with the scenery or something."

When we arrived at the grand ballroom of a local hotel, the first things we noticed were a half-dozen young lovelies serving drinks from three gigantic punch bowls. The punch was at least 100 proof (that seems to be the real secret to talent recruitment); and you couldn't even take a short sip from your glass without some attentive pusher refilling it. Things loosened up fast; and it was getting to be quite a swinging affair when the chairwoman took her spot at the microphone on stage and introduced the straight-from-New York producer and director. Let's call him Bobbie Lyon. That isn't his real name; but, then, I'm not sure that what he told us was his real name. He was a bundle of talent, though. He could sing, dance, tell jokes and motivate. As I watched him give his opening spiel, I was reminded of that barker who once sold gasoline on the old Milton Berle Show. Before I really knew what had happened, I had signed up for two humorous skits, a specialty song and dance act, and had volunteered for the dancing chorus.

This was a far cry, I must admit, from just helping move a few chairs around behind the scenes; but that positive pitchman made show business sound like the easiest thing in the world. "If you can count to four, you can do our simple dance routines," he explained. "You don't have to carry a tune to sing with us. You can just talk the words. Simple as can be. In our comedy routines, all you have to learn is a sentence or two."

Not only did he tell us how easy it was, he showed us. He took a half dozen of us prospective scenery movers and within two minutes had us doing a quite complicated dance routine. Three steps to the left. Three to the right and kick, kick, kick. Then we shouted the words from *When the Saints Come Marchin' In,* and were positively convinced that those people who make their living in show business are a bunch of thieves. There was nothing to it. Just count one-two-three and shout . . . "Oh, when the saints . . ." We were ready for Broadway. And we still had three glorious weeks of happy, happy rehearsals ahead. What could be easier than that?

However, with sobriety came fear and the dire realization that we had committed ourselves to an uneasy way of life. Four rehearsals for two weeks and then almost daily until opening night.

Bobbie Lyon's effervescence at rehearsals was not nearly as heady as the spiked punch we had gargled at the tryout; and it took only a few minutes at that first dance rehearsal to discover that we would have to do far more than merely count to three to succeed. We would have to do one hell of a lot of high counting, high kicking and even a little miracle working if we expected to avoid falling flat on our high hopes when the curtain went up opening night. "That's fine. That's fine. Just great," Bobbie would keep yelling, though our dance numbers had the split-second timing of a mob trying to file out of a football stadium after a losing game.

At the chorus rehearsal, we received the words we were expected to shout. "Just learn the words," Bobbie explained. But, when we got down to it, learning the words to half-a-dozen complicated songs became a real chore.

The humor skits were simply old vaudeville routines; and if you could memorize half-a-dozen short lines, you were in. The real problem was that we were onstage doing humor skits for one big reason — to pace the show while the singers and dancers changed costumes. It was at the dress rehearsal that this terrifying truth struck me. I would have to dress one way for a specialty act or a skit and then be ready for the next thing that came onstage. All I had to do was fill in while others changed and then suddenly appear a couple of seconds later in a different outfit, ready to dance onstage with a group.

A dress rehearsal really lets a guy find out who his real friends are. I was running around explaining my problem to everyone in sight, but for some reason no one responded with the kindness and understanding I so desperately sought. Everyone was busy trying to remember what he was supposed to do. Every set of lips was busily engaged in a conversation with its owner, rehearsing lines, repeating words to songs, counting, counting, counting, and trying to remember whether to turn right or left.

I finally worked it out for myself. I compromised on half costumes for each scene. I was half dressed for each number — a little from the old scene and a little from the new and possibly a smattering of the scene to come — a clown suit tucked casually under my dressy tuxedo, a comic tie hidden discreetly under the back of my shirt collar.

And then, suddenly, it was happening. The audience was ready; but it was all too clear to everyone concerned that we were not. The chorus sounded like a bunch of misguided mumbles chanting out only half-learned lyrics. The dance line looked like a beginning football team muffing a key play from scrimmage. The specialty acts looked glitteringly unspecial. The chorus costumes were ravishing, but the dancers looked tired.

As the band began the overture, we joined together in a united belief that our own Nuremberg Trial was about to begin. We collectively hated Bobbie Lyon, the coward, who refused to come onstage with us, giving the flimsy excuse that it was our show, not his.

Then the curtain went up and magic happened. The lights brought the costumes alive; and somehow a transfusion of talent transfigured our poor offering into an act of inspiration. For when the curtain came down after the opening number, the applause was a symphony to our eager ears. From that instant there was no stopping our

victory. Our subconscious minds freely fed out the words to our lips, and the right steps to our tingling feet. We sang out; and we danced, oh, how we danced and joked and smiled and bowed to the resounding applause and bowed again. Our hate for so-called Bobbie Lyon had burst into love and pride and devotion. And our hearts became so full that some of us feared that that very night we might need that cardiac arrest cart which we had all worked so hard to buy.

Sparked with our new-found confidence and the terrific newspaper reviews, we outdid ourselves in our second and final performance. And after the final act, we packed the costumes and headed for the Victory Party that would be followed the next morning at 11 a.m. by a Gin-fizz Brunch.

Every community should have at least one annual follies. It makes willing scenery movers into audience captivators, and somehow the world is a little nicer place when the final curtain falls.

Deliverin'

"Daniel," I cried upstairs with not just a little irritation creeping into my voice, "Mrs. Klingman just called and said you missed her house tonight. I don't know what's wrong. You're always getting calls. When I was a kid with a paper route, nobody ever called our house."

Daniel ambled slowly down the stairs and patiently replied, "And you didn't have a telephone either, dad. Maybe that helped."

"I don't know why you can't deliver those papers right."

"Speaking of delivering papers right, dad, how would you like to sub for me tomorrow morning? Dennis wants me to camp out overnight with him. I could . . . ah . . . just go over the route with you, and I'm sure you could handle it."

"Can't you get Corky? He does a good job."

"He's visiting his aunt this weekend."

"But that's the morning edition, Dan."

"It's Saturday, dad. The lightest paper of the week. Nothing to it. Will you help me out?"

I melted with his warmth. "Why not?" I finally agreed. "There's nothing to delivering a paper route."

"Let's go over the deliveries," Daniel suggested. "I'll show you how to save a few steps."

"Steps?" I asked. "Can't I just ride your bike down the center of the street and let 'em fly?" I chuckled. "I remember how I could do my whole route in 11 minutes. Those papers really zinged through the air. And I kept a kind of running score — one point if it landed on the porch, three if it landed in the bushes and a bonus of ten extra points if it landed up on the roof. I was some kind of an all-time high scorer."

"We hand-deliver them now, dad. We put them in the mailboxes and inside the storm doors and things like that."

"You kids need a union," I suggested.

"It's not so bad. Here, I'll show you how it goes."

Daniel ran through the route. This one in the mailbox, another inside the door. "And this one you go up three flights of steps and leave it on the table."

"Three flights?" I asked. "Do they tip you good for that?"

Daniel sighed patiently. "Dad, if they could afford to tip me, they wouldn't live three flights up. Now, here, you cut through the alley and catch two houses on this other street. Then back and . . ."

"I cut through the alley?" I asked.

"Nobody's up to see you that time of morning. Don't worry about it, dad."

"What's this 14 mean?"

"That's the big house for the old ladies. You leave 14 papers in the chair on the front porch. If you tap on the front window, you'll attract the attention of four or five of the old ladies in the living room; and if you smile and wave at them they appreciate it because they don't see too many visitors. So if you think of it, tap."

"Sure, Dan, I'll tap and smile and wave. I'll remember."

Dan smiled. But as he looked back at the list, the smile disappeared. "At 216, you've got to look out for a dog. They've got this big sign in the yard, 'Beware of Vicious Dog', and, dad, they aren't kidding!"

"Maybe you'd better get your mom to deliver this," I suggested.

"Mom?" he asked.

"Sure, your mom. You know, Dan. She's got a way with dogs."

"You do it. You're long on experience and know-how."

I felt trapped. "Any other tips?" I asked.

"Dad," he continued, "remember, you have to have the whole route delivered by 8 o'clock."

"Sure. No sweat. Just wipe the whole thing out of your mind, Dan. The route is in good hands. Don't worry about it. Say, what's this one with the five stars in front of it, Dan?"

Dan hesitated a little and then finally admitted, "He owes me for five weeks."

"Five weeks," I stormed. "What kind of a deadbeat would owe a newspaper boy for five weeks. Cut him off, Dan."

Dan smiled that darn smile of his that goes clear through you. "I can't do that, dad. That guy's been sick. And with all that time in bed, the newspaper is something he looks forward to every day. I just keep his card up-to-date out of my tip money. It makes me feel good, dad."

"That makes me feel good, too, Dan," I admitted.

We shook hands; and when the alarm went off the next morning, I had the feeling that I'd been had. How did he talk me into giving up the only morning in the week that I can sleep in? Well, he'd done it. And there I was with that list of numbers, stumbling around in the dark, trying to find those darn house numbers that either weren't there at all or, at least, were well hidden. I slowly struggled along with that sackful of papers that suddenly seemed to weigh at least a total ton, and did my best to figure out the strange house-numbering system. The only address I was really certain of was the one with the dog. Thank heaven, that dog at 216 was inside. But his bark sent a chill of terror up my spine.

At that home for the old ladies, I tapped on the window and, sure enough, there were five of them, dressed and looking very much as if they'd gotten up early just to answer that tap with their friendly smiles. They looked a little surprised to see me, but they smiled anyway and waved; and, somehow, I was glad I'd climbed out of bed that morning, too.

When I finally completed the route, third-floor delivery and all, I slumped down exhausted at the kitchen table, only to hear the telephone ring. It was Mrs. Klingman. I was certain I'd delivered her paper. And then Mr. Jennings called, and Mrs. Fenner, and Sam Browning. That darn thing kept ringing off the hook for the next two hours. I soon ran out of papers and had to buy 10 extras from the corner stand. But I still can't figure it out, because I know that I delivered a paper to every single house on that list.

Dan returned home early that evening. "How'd it go, dad?" he asked.

"Nothing to it," I lied. "Nothing to it at all. Got every house O.K." I added silently to myself, ". . . finally."

"How about helping me collect, then?" he asked.

"No, Dan. I'm pretty busy. I've got things to do. Count me out."

"O.K., dad," he said, "but since I'm collecting, how about paying me right now for our paper?"

"Swell," I said. I reached into my pocket and took out a dollar. Then I thought about it and reached in again.

"What's the extra buck for, pa?" he asked. "Do you want to pay ahead?"

I looked up at my six-foot-one, fifteen-year-old wonder boy and grinned. "No, Dan. Not to pay ahead. That's a tip. I guess you deserve it. There's more to that paper business than the average guy thinks about. Take that buck, Dan; and, say, why don't you buy a little hamburger for that dog at 216?"

Skip a Little

Just last week, as I was walking on one of our downtown streets, I felt an uncontrollable urge to skip. So I did. It felt so good I did it again; only this time I did a double skip. I smiled to myself over what I had accomplished. A double skip right in the heart of traffic is something to be long remembered.

Skipping in downtown pedestrian traffic is out of the ordinary. But, in a way, it is what a good, honest Christian ought to do in today's world. Skipping is fun and so is clean Christian living. Of course, you have to develop the courage to admit what you are doing when someone notices you. You have to look your friends in the eye and say: "I'm staying away from that movie because it is indecent," or, "That course of action isn't right, and so it's not for me."

When I was a GI, I used to do that skipping business every now and then just to retain my sanity. I'd purposely get out of step when we were marching. I looked like a Yankee Gomer Pyle. I'd skip out of step and then skip back in; it gave me a marvelous feeling of freedom. Occasionally, our drill sergeant would yell out: "Fettig, get in step," and I'd do it fast enough. But I knew that at any time I so desired, I could skip again and be an individual, even in a drill team.

Now, I don't recommend group skipping; imagine, if you can, a drill team that skips in unison. But I do recommend individual skips now and then. Conformity at a high level for all is fine; but — let's face it — most of us lower our standard when we simply conform.

I love to see an individual break out of the mold — to do something useful for himself or others. I think that it is patriotic to burst through the ordinary, because that is what America is all about. Freedom of speech, press, religion . . . what are these rights if we don't exercise them? Who needs them if they are not practiced? If a man can't and won't be himself, then he might as well be a puppet. If a man doesn't act in a free manner, then possibly he doesn't deserve his freedom.

Take freedom of religion, for example. It gives you the right to act in a moral way in everything you do. I don't mean narrow-mindedly or stiffly. I don't suggest that you go through life with a sad face, seeing evil in everything under the sun. I mean that you should act with integrity. Use the foundation of your religion's morality in everything you do. Practice your freedom of religion by living within the standards of your chosen faith.

Skipping is just a little thing, but I like to do everything a little differently now and then. I like to break out of the ordinary in eating, sleeping and even walking. I try to read a different kind of book now and then — in a new field I haven't yet explored.

I have bought loud ties on occasion. I even tie my shoes a little differently from time to time. And I feel that this has made my life more interesting. Doing things by habit makes them lose their significance. Live by habit, and all life loses its meaning.

Try getting over to Europe or Asia or maybe to a small island in the Caribbean. Notice how everything around you is interesting and exciting? Maybe it isn't to the natives, but to you it is. It is so different. Everything is a new experience and, therefore, you are free of habit-living.

Skip, and tear off a whole hunk of this wonderful thing we call living, but do it morally. Don't run away from life in an effort to escape reality. If reality leaves much to be desired, then pitch in and change it for the better. Don't try to drink or smoke or dream your way through life. Face it. Test it. Then fill your cup with the experiences that are so much more wonderful when they are tasted within the bounds of your religion's morality.

Try skipping in the heart of town. Do a hop if you dare. Step out. Change a little for the better. Take a different route on your daily trips. Vary your eating habits. Meet new people drink in all the life that surrounds you. Break out a little. Don't try to skip life. Skip through it.

The Name Game

Naming your new baby can be one of the most rewarding experiences in the world, provided you name your baby after a very rich relative who is on the brink of death. Otherwise, the job of naming your offspring can be like working a *New York Times* Sunday crossword puzzle without a dictionary, or fighting World War II barehanded.

Decisions. Decisions. Decisions. With modern medical science, a married couple now has to decide first if and when they want a little darling, and once the decision is made and the deed is done and that little bundle of heaven is on his way, then your thinking begins. What should we name the baby?

"If it is a boy, we'll name him after my father," I suggested.

"You were named after your father," my wife Ruth reminded me. "In other words, you'd want to name our son after you."

"Well, you could put it that way," I admitted, "but I didn't want to appear vain."

Since Ruth likes my father, she agreed. Our only problem would come if the child were a girl.

It seems so wrong to me that parents should be saddled with the responsibility of naming their children. It would be so simple if they merely came out of the womb with a tag like those revelers wear at conventions. You know. Tags that say things like, "Hello. My name is Zeke Browning. What's yours?"

Names are important. A person's position in life can be determined by his name. Especially in school. Everything, and I mean everything, is done alphabetically. We had a girl in our class named Zelda Zwayback, and poor Zelda never got in on anything. We did everything alphabetically, and by the time they got to the XYZ's, the bell always rang. When Zelda was just 14 years old, her kidneys conked out on her.

Our little bundle of feminine bliss came zipping out right on time, and we suddenly realized that we were faced with the naming problem. Being a born researcher at heart, I raced over to the library and took out three books on naming girls. All three books were by different authors, and all three listed the exact same names. But, after all, how original can an author get in writing a book on girls' names? Maybe if he was a spirited penman, he might make up a few names just to enlarge the book. (I did notice that all of the books were rather thin.) Think of the fun in creating new names and then making up meanings for them. How about Oniony, for example? Definition: Bermudian name meaning misty-eyed. An author could change the naming habits of the whole nation if he

had the time and imagination.

A chore faced my weak wife and me. I took my thin names' book right up to the hospital room, together with a sweet-smelling bunch of flowers and greeted my wife with, "Hello, my love. Ready to play the name game?"

"Ready," she replied. "How is it played?"

"Simple," I said. "I'll mention some names, and you see how they hit you. But first we both have to remember that we have certain mental fixations about names. It isn't that we don't like the sound of certain names; it is just that they bring to mind certain people, and if we don't like those people, we tend to dislike their names. I'll go down the list, and you let me know how you like them."

"Sounds easy," she said brightly. "We'll have a name in no time that way."

"Of course. Now here we go. Abigail?" I said brightly.

She made no comment, just gave me a blank stare, so I continued, "Alberta?"

Nothing.

"Amy?"

"We already have one Amy at home," she reminded me.

"I know that," I said, "I just thought I'd see if you still liked the name. Anastasia?"

"That sounds like the Mafia," she said.

"Anne?"

"No, too much like Nancy. We have a Nancy, remember?"

"Honestly, Ruth, I know our children's names. You don't have to keep reminding me. I'm helping to take care of them while you are here. In addition to that, I have been supporting them and trying to be a good father to them. I know their names; I type it on all those income-tax forms every year. Now, how about Barbara?"

"No," she said, "That is our new niece's name."

"Belinda?" I asked.

"No, skip those offbeat names, please."

"O.K., here's a cute name. Bridget."

"Yech . . . Bardot. No."

"Candace?"

"Sounds like a card game. Have you been playing poker with the boys while I'm in here?"

"I've been taking care of our little dears," I said, "and I assume you don't want a Candace in the family?"

"You assume right," she smiled brightly and shifted her position in bed, trying once more to get comfortable. "Now what is next?"

"Constance? Cynthia?"

"Both are too old-fashioned or too modern, I forget which."

"Dale?"

"Sounds like a Roy Rogers movie. What's next?"

"Donna," I smiled.

She frowned. "Donna Day," she said. "Remember how you kissed Donna Day at that New Year's party? It was positively disgusting."

"To you maybe, but not to me. I wasn't disgusted at all. Besides, it was just a little friendly kiss."

"Friendly!" she cried out. "Boy, people can almost have babies being that friendly."

"You're exaggerating," I argued. "I just gave her a little peck on the cheek. Now I assume you don't want a Donna around, so I'll proceed. Eugenia?"

"That sounds like a name some father made up when he couldn't get a Eugene. I don't like any of those boys' names with an 'ia' tacked on for frosting. What now?"

"Faith?"

"No," she said, "and not Hope or Charity either."

"Why don't you rest a while, dear? I don't want to get you upset over a simple thing like naming a baby. I can come back later."

"Don't you dare leave," she said. "We are going to get this baby named. I'll try to be a little happier about the whole thing." She smiled, patted my hand affectionately and I tried again.

"Francine?"

"Too foreign sounding."

"Gail?"

"Too breezy."

"Gloria?"

"Gloria Hallelujah!" she laughed and so did I.

"Irene?"

"Goodnight," she said.

"What do you mean, goodnight? Visiting hours aren't over. I thought you wanted to get this settled."

"The song," she explained, "remember? Goodnight, Irene, goodnight, Irene, I'll see you in my dreams."

I brightened. "Sure. In the army we used to sing it, "Goodnight, Irene, my sex machine, I'll see you in my dreams."

"Let's not get dirty. What is the next name?"

"Jacqueline? I know. That's our dog's name. We couldn't stand two of those in the family. How about Jane?"

"Too plain."

"Juliet?"

"We don't have a balcony," she reminded.

"Karen?"

She glowed.

"No," I said, "your sister's name is Karen. No offense, but it wouldn't be right. Kate?"

"Kiss me." And she waited dramatically. I did.

Finally, I said, "You're funny; I just bet you can make up a joke for every name I read. You're a riot. Maybe we should just name our baby Laughing Girl."

"I'm sorry," she said. "I'm really trying, but I feel kind of light-headed right now."

"That's normal," I said.

"You mean that it is normal after my having a baby and all?" she asked.

"No. I mean that light-headed is normal for you, dear. Now, how about Lisa?"

"I like that," she said.

I didn't. "The child next-door is named Lisa." Enough said. "Lilly?"

"And she could be a flower child."

"Loretta? Lucy?"

"I love Lucy."

"Margaret?"

"A princess. Too regal."

"Marsha?"

"Sounds too swampy."

"Nora?" Again, I got that frozen look.

"You'd like that, wouldn't you?" she said. "You'd like to name her Nora so she could remind you of that sexy secretary you used to date."

"I'd completely forgotten her. Besides, I only took her out once and that was long before I even met you. And she wasn't sexy."

"You'd like to call her Nora and . . ."

"Olivia," I shouted. "What about Olivia?"

"It sounds like something you'd drop in a martini."

"Penelope?"

"A century too late."

"Prudence?"

"Sounds like a virtue, not a name."

"Roberta? Rosalie?"

A shake of the head for each.

I was getting mighty tired of reading names and said so. "You keep shaking your head. Why don't you try to think positive thoughts? Why don't you say, 'Yes, I'm going to find a very pretty name for our daughter, and right now.' Go ahead. Say it."

"Don't try that silly positive-thinking routine on me," she said. "I'm trying. I'm really trying. Now what is the next name?"

"Rosemary," I said. "I like Rosemary."

"But we already vetoed that."

"No, that was Rosalie. I'm not trying to trick you with subtle repetition or anything. Well, how about Shelly? Stephanie? Suzanne? Theodora? Tina? Valerie?" I threw the book down disgustedly. "You aren't even listening. Let's just call her Baby Girl Fettig. When she reaches legal age she can pick her own darn name. Get some sleep, dear, and I will too. It's been a rough, tiring experience for both of us." I walked to the door, only to hear Ruth's faint call.

"Yes?" I asked. "What name do like? Me? I like Rosemary. Huh? With and 'ie' instead of of 'y'? Great. Rosemarie. I love it. You do too? Great. Swell. Gee, honey, it wasn't hard was it? Easy. There is really nothing to picking a name for people who get along as well as we do."

Church Full of Love

This evening at 7 o'clock Mass, our church was a house full of love. Love, yes, and joy, much joy. And pride and understanding and generosity and hope.

Strangely, Father talked about money; and you know how people hate to hear about that in church. He spoke about our debt and the fact that we will have to make some real effort if we hope to keep our Catholic schools running. And yet he communicated hope and love. Maybe that is what made it so acceptable.

Seven o'clock Mass on Saturday is a relaxed, informal situation. Nobody worries too much about formal dress. I'd been busy all day and hadn't bothered to shave. I was wearing my corduroy pants and my red velour shirt; and when my usher friend, Gene, signaled to me that he'd like help with the collection, I nodded agreement. I felt comfortable in my casual clothing.

When I saw the look of love and understanding on Father's face as he explained finances and collections and other things that pastors simply must discuss at times, I resolved to try a bit harder to make his job easier. I decided that a couple more dollars a week wouldn't hurt our family budget, what with my cost-of-living raise and all. Then I walked to the rear of the church and picked up my collection basket.

I guess I first noticed the atmosphere of love in the voices of the young people as they sang to the beat of a guitar, "Hear, O Lord." I found myself smiling as I sang along with them. There was love, too, in the smile of our associate pastor as he sang himself down the aisle. (Father sings with real gusto.) And it was impossible to miss the love of our pastor as he asked us for help in saving our schools.

When I passed the basket, quite a number of $5 bills appeared; $1 bills were all I'd ever noticed before. Even the children wore happy smiles as they dropped their pennies and nickels in the basket. Even the Korean orphans, adopted several years ago by one of the families in the parish, were smiling confidently. I remember when they first arrived, nearly starved and terrified by their new surroundings. But the love and caring had changed all of that.

The older people, too, seemed to enjoy singing the young people's songs. When I reached the vestibule where the contents of all the baskets are poured into one, I met the young black couple who was about to begin the offertory procession. It was easy to see the real joy on their faces as they prepared to represent the entire community on this occasion. There was dignified pride in their carriage — no fear or anger, just love. Much love.

Back at my seat with my family, I looked about and marveled at how the Catholic Church has changed in the past decade. No longer do we listen to the recitation of the Latin Mass; we now celebrate it in our native tongue. The Communion railing has disappeared, so that there is real contact with the priest who now faces us at an altar brought forward to meet our needs. New songs ring from the rafters, and a new spirit breathes in the church.

When the priest spoke the words, "Let us offer each other a sign of peace," I suddenly realized what had really changed. I greeted my wife, and then turned to shake hands with the man beside me. "The Lord's peace be with you, brother," he said; and I replied, "And with you, brother." A black man in the pew behind me smiled and held out his hand; and I felt such joy as I took it and offered him words of peace. Then the man ahead turned, and, as each of us extended his hand, I knew that we were at last beginning to reach each other on a one-to-one basis. We were finally becoming neighbors, a loving community joined in the joy of Jesus, sharing the knowledge that there is joy in reaching out to our fellow-man by saying, "Come inside."

When Mass officially ended, actually it had only begun, because outside the church the warmth that filled our hearts still prevailed; and hundreds of people who had somehow been too busy before suddenly recognized each other and waved and smiled and shook hands and exchanged words of joy. Even on the parking lot not an angry horn was blown; people had time to let their neighbors go first. The young and the old greeted each other as if there were no such thing as a generation gap.

This evening at the 7 o'clock Mass, our church was a house full of love, and I'm so very grateful that I was a part of it.

Life Is for Cheering

It was during the fourth quarter of our local high school's final basketball game that I caught myself jumping up and down and screaming with delight, "Two, two, two." We'd scored another two points to put us ahead; and at that moment, all was right with the world. I personally knew four of the boys out on the court and was so choked up and involved with what was going on that I had to jump up and scream just to let my joy run over.

Our parish conducted a fund-raising drive last year. We were shooting for a goal of $200,000. We needed that minimum in additional income for the next three years if we hoped to keep our Catholic school system running. At the Wednesday night meeting, all of the workers were there to report on their returns. It was still early in the drive, with only a little over half of the families contacted; but our efforts thus far had produced a grand total of $262,000. Imagine, over a quarter of a million dollars in pledges already; and when we had first tackled this mountain, we hadn't even dreamt of reaching the top. When they announced that figure, a cheer went up from every person there. We cheered and turned grinning to our neighbors to shake hands and offer each other congratulations and good wishes. Right then, each one of us made a personal resolution to go out and finish the drive with even more gusto than we'd had before. We'd make that final total soar now, for each one of us knew that God was making us dynamic salesmen and merging us into a winning team. So, together, we cheered the miracle that was happening.

And then there was the follies. A hospital auxiliary sponsored a variety show to raise money to buy a special piece of heart equipment for the hospital. First, there had been the talent search and the recruitment of workers; next, the rehearsals which consumed many precious moments of the busy people involved; then the search for advertisers, the ticket sales and the promotions; and finally the applause of the crowd and the jubilant relief of the cast after the final performance. Ours was a cheer of joy that came with doing, a yell to celebrate another victory over apathy.

Meanwhile, dozens of people are busily involved at the Civic Theater turning out wonderful productions. The Civic Art Center continues to hold well-attended classes in all types of art. A concert orchestra rehearses daily, as well as several high-school bands and a wonderful choir. Over at the Y there is family volleyball and at the Civic Recreation Building there is swimming for the whole family. And at the Community College, over 50 different classes are offered each weekday evening.

People are busy in their churches and over at the Junior Achievement building. Throughout the city, people attend meetings of Alcoholics Anonymous, Narcotics Anonymous, Weight Watchers and Parents without Partners.

Somewhere, though, right in the middle of all this activity, there are those pathetic creatures who yawn, sigh and say, "There's nothin' to do in this lousy city." And among them can be counted some of the restless young: "What else is there to do in this town but turn to drugs? There's just nothin' else happening here."

What it all boils down to is this: There is really never anything to do for those who do nothing. For whatever you do from the position of non-involvement is non-involving. Life is a real bore if you don't live it, just as swimming doesn't make sense unless you get into the water. And life was made for jumping up and cheering.

Human nature makes people say "no" first. No, I'm too busy. I want to see that TV show, "Father Knows Nothin'." It is so much easier to sit and watch the boob tube than it is to get up and do something. And yet the difference between actually becoming involved in something and just standing on the fringe watching is the difference between being truly *alive* and just being. Involvement is what makes life worth living. And when you put it all together and really become involved in the life around you, your own life becomes exciting. You find more and more moments when you are jumping up and down and cheering and saying to yourself, "Gosh, I'm glad I'm alive. I'm so proud of my team — our team. Our family, our Church, our city, our country."

But the person who sits on the fringe and does nothing only becomes more and more unhappy and disillusioned. He sits alone in his confusion and continually asks, "Why isn't there anything to do in this city? What's wrong with this world?"

Now, what about you? When is the last time you jumped up and down with excitement? Are you getting old before your time? Are you one of those unforturnate "do-nothing" creatures who lies in bed in the morning and wonders if it is worth the effort to go on living? Nothing to do? Why, there is everything to do; and other people are doing it. This world would be such a better place if only the "do-nothings" would get busy and do something.

The Lord had a purpose in populating this world. Every creature was put on this earth for a reason, a purpose, a mission, a cause for his or her existence; and if any one of us fails to perform that mission, then it will go undone for all eternity. We all have our "things" to do, and if we would perform, this world would function in symphony. Songs are going unsung, good deeds undone. Those in need of comfort go uncomforted. Potential leaders fail to lead. Creators fail to create. Problem-solvers sit in apathy as crises go unresolved. The time has come in the world when we all must get up and do our thing if we hope to survive.

Once again, what about you? What are your talents? How did God mean for you to shine? Certainly, God didn't plan for 200 million people to excel at television watching. He didn't plan life to be a spectator sport. God meant for all of us to contribute; and it is time for us to make that contribution in the form of a total commitment to life.

Think of how many hours you spend each day doing virtually nothing. Couldn't you fit a worthwhile activity into that time. And examine those hours in which you are occupied, too. How many hours do you devote to your fellow-man? How many to the improvement of the society in which you live? What are *you* doing?

Life is a yell-out, jump-up-and-down thing for those who accept the challenge. Life is beautiful and rewarding, but only for those who earn its rewards through the involvement in the world around them.

Growth Unlimited Catalog

JUST SAY YES

Just say, "Yes,"
To believing you're special.
Just say, "Yes,"
To being kind.
Just say, "Yes,"
To caring for others.
Just say, "Yes,"
To improving your mind.

Just say, "Yes,"
To trying harder.
Just say, "Yes,"
To hanging in.
Just say, "Yes,"
To growing daily.
Just say, "Yes,"
To learning to win.

Just say, "Hey there
I'm somebody
And you are too.
Let's do our best."
Stand up! Listen,
To what is right
Respect yourself
And just say, "Yes!"

by Art Fettig

The Three Robots Help Kids Say "YES" To Positive Living

> *"Here is one of the best books I have seen to teach children the principles of positive thinking, health and happinesss. Art Fettig has done a charming and creative work in 'The Three Robots' and adults will like it too. I know for I like it tremendously."*
>
> Dr. Norman Vincent Peale – Author of the Power of Positive Thinking

The Three Robots Just Say Yes Kit

"What a delightful book! And I love what 'Pos' does and the beautiful lesson it leaves!"
Robert Schuller – Pastor, Crystal Cathedral

2 Great Books

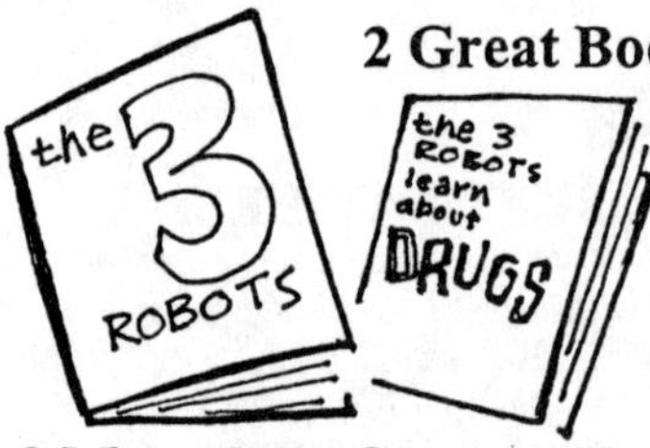

The Three Robots
Teaches how to be happy and healthy. (CHB-1)

The Three Robots Learn About Drugs
Saying "No" to drugs, "Yes" to positive living and realizing that you are "somebody special." (CHB-7)

3 Marvelous Cassette Tapes

The Three Robots–the book narrated
Your children will listen again and again. (CHT-1)

The Three Robots Learn About Drugs
An excellent narration of the book. (CHT-7)

The Just Say Yes Rap & Somebody
Features singer Paul Lee Marr. Kids love it and it reinforces positive values. (CHT-8)

1 Just Say Yes Activity Book

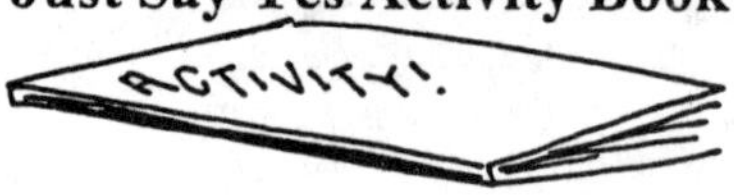

Easy to use, it gives you a ten week action program that builds self-esteem and creates life changing, positive values. (CHB-8)

10 Pos Stickers, An Achievement Card, and an "I'm a Pos" Pin

A $34.20 Value... Special – Just $29.95 (CHYK-1)

(Add $3 Shipping)

The Three Robots Books and Tapes Also Sold Individually

Books	$3.95
Work Books	$5.95
Tapes	$5.95

Wayne Dyer:
"My children love these books. They learn positive attitudes and loving reactions to life. What greater testimonial could you ask?"

The Three Robots Just Say Yes Kit is great for parents to use in the home with their children and it can be used in classrooms too. Thousands of children have already benefited from this powerful program. Don't Delay!

Give your kids that rare gift of a Positive Attitude and a sense of values that will last them a lifetime.

THE THREE ROBOTS SUCCESS KIT

Keep that positive spirit alive with your kids with more great ideas from The Three Robots!

4 More Great Books

The Three Robots Find a Grandpa
This book teaches how to become loveable, loving yourself, loving others and being loved in return. (CHB-4)

The Three Robots And The Sandstorm
Kids learn about teamwork and overcoming setbacks and disabilities. (CHB-2)

The Three Robots Discover Their Pos-Abilities
A unique 8 Step Goal Setting Process that works with people of all ages. (CHB-3)

Remembering—A book for kids to help them teach their parents to remember. Makes learning and remembering easier. (CHB-6)

The Three Robots Activity Book

More than just pictures to color, this unique collection of practical ideas helps parents and teachers focus the child's energy on life changing, positive values. (CHB-5)

10 Pos Stickers, an Achievement Card and an "I'm a Pos" pin

Four Fantastic Tapes

You receive cassette tape narrations of all four of the above great books. Kids listen to the tape again and again, reinforcing these powerful, concepts in their subconscious minds. Helps to overcome the bombardment of negativism they are exposed to daily. (CHT-2-3-4-6)

Everything Above! A $48.05 Value Now Just $39.95! (CHSK-1)

Why wait until your children are grown up and accidentally stumble upon success concepts? Teach them now about success and happiness. As a bonus you will learn these powerful success principles as you share them with your children.

"The Three Robots is a story for kids–but adults need the message too. It's simple, clear, direct, motivational and much needed in our society. I believe it will help kids of all ages."

Zig Ziglar, the World's #1 Motivation Speaker

the POS PARENTING Package

"Art Fettig, in his new book The Three Robots, is filling a great need. Many young children blame a 'bad day' on a parent or teacher–even the weather! To teach children that no one can give them happiness and that they will determine whether they have a happy or a sad day, is to teach them one of the most important lessons in life."

Marilyn VanDerbur – Noted educator and former Miss America

2 Great Books

Pos Parenting – A guide to greatness, with 25 keys for building your child's positive self-esteeem. In America today we are experiencing an epidemic of low self-esteem. The symptoms are evident everywhere. Low school grades, lack of friendships, TV addiction, drug abuse, promiscuity; yes, even the highest teenage suicide rate in the world. This book addresses the problem and offers suggestions on how you can build not only your child's self-esteem but your own as well. (PRB-1)

It Only Hurts When I Frown – A series of humorous-serious sketches on family relations and on the joy of raising 4 children. Hilarious, real and heart touching. It will make you laugh and nod your head and say, "Yes, I've been there too." (PRB-2)

A Stirring 2 Tape Audio Program

Positive Parenting. Taped live for an audience of concerned parents. You'll discover that you are not alone and that raising children today takes a special person with a special commitment. You'll laugh and no doubt you will cry, but most important, you will probably do a better job of parenting after hearing this touching program. (PRA-1)

A $33.90 Value – Special Just $29.95 (PRC-1)

Fantastic Combination Offer

Get All Three Combinations At A Remarkable Savings

Yes, we'd like you to benefit from all of our products created for parents and children. You receive all three combinations, The Three Robot Just Say Yes Kit (a $34.20 value), The Three Robot Success Course (a $48.05 value), and the Pos Parenting Package (a $33.90 value), **a total retail value of $116.16, all for just $79.95**, plus $5 shipping. (PRC-2)

When you buy the complete package we will include an attractive vinyl 8-pack album for the tapes.

Unfortunately, today, most people learn about success and happiness in some form of rehabiliation program, that is, if they survive.

The question you must ask yourself is this, "Do I want my children to learn that they are special, wonderful, unique individuals now or do I want them to discover it after they have really made a mess of their lives?"

This valuable combination of great life changing ideas and techniques are yours just for the asking at a price that anyone can afford.

Just call us at 1-800-441-7676 right now and get started immediately on a success program that will not only touch your child's life but yours as well.

To order just call us, or if you prefer you can send your check or money order to Growth Unlimited Inc., 36 Fairview, Battle Creek, Michigan, 49017. Our FAX Number is 616-965-4522. Yes, we take Visa, Master Card or American Express.

Call us at 1-800-441-7676 Today!

A $116.16 Value – Special Just $79.95 (PRC-2)

(Add $5 Shipping)

"It captures the world of childhood imagination beautifully"
Art Linkletter, author of Kids Say the Darndest Things

The Platinum Rule — The age old secret to happiness and prosperity

"It is terrific!" – *W. Clement Stone* "Wonderful message" – *Og Mandino*

"The Platinum Rule is great. And it's needed too" – *Dr. Norman Viucent Peale*

Paperback Edition (PDB-3) $5.95
Special Hardcover Autographed Edition (PDB-3H) $12.95
Please add $3 shipping

Love is the Target — An answer for troubled Americans, today

This little book will provide you with the answer you seek to live a happier, healthier, more productive life.

Paperback (LTB) $5.95

Now available on video and audio tape.

Taped live with a great audience, this 44 minute presentation will entertain and inspire you.

Audio Tape (LTT) $9.95
Video Tape (LTV) $39.95

A $51.85 Value
Just $40!

Super Special **– Get all three!**
The book, the audio and the video tapes for just (LTC) $40.00

Serenity! Serenity!—Living The Serenity Prayer

One man's quest for serenity, acceptance and courage.

Paperback (SSB) $5.95

Coming Soon

Audio and Video Tapes of both The Platinum Rule and Serenity! Serenity! To be recorded with a live audience, Art Fettig's presentations have the fire and the passion that will reach you and touch your life. Call or write for information from Growth Unlimited Inc., 36 Fairview, Battle Creek, MI, 49017. Call 1-800-441-7676!

Art Fettig is accepting a limited number of speaking engagements to help spread the powerful message contained in his book Love is the Target. For more information on rates and availability call 1-800-441-7676.

How to Hold an Audience in the Hollow of Your Hand
Art Fettig, veteran of nearly 4,000 professional speeches reveals the techniques of the top professionals. 7 powerful ways to win an audience in the first 5 minutes and 11 techniques to keep them listening. A proven winner. (PSB-1, $9.95)

Anatomy of a Speech
Discover how to create exciting, powerful, winning speeches using the vignette style of speech construction. Save hours and improve your presentations immediately. (PSBK-1, $3.95)

The Art of Public Speaking
Learn to use humor effectively. How to win an audience, how to stack the odds in your favor. Proven techniques demonstrated by top professional speakers, recorded at live presentations. 4-Tape Album,.(PSA-1, $49.95)

The Best Verse of Art Fettig and Friends
Camera ready copy of Art Fettig's most popular verses. Includes Growth, Self-Esteem Credo, Just Say Yes, Teacher-Teacher, My Brother Joe and many others. (BV-1, $3.95)

Selling Lucky
By applying the sensational sales methods revealed in this book, you'll achieve more in your business, job or personal relationships. A no-holds barred look at what it takes to be a great salesperson. (SLB-1, $9.95)

Selling Luckier Yet
This companion volume to "Selling Lucky" is full of interesting anecdotes, personal sales strategies and many new ways to close that sale. (SLB-2, $5.95)

Mentor: Secret of the Ages
Now, you'll be introduced to your own personal mentor, your "friend in need" in time of crisis. Whenever you want, you'll be able to turn to this written masterpiece for guidance and comfort. Hardcover (PDB-1, $9.95), Cassette (PDT-1, $9.95) or both (PDC-1, $15.95)

The Art of Greatness
Unlock the "success consciousness" that lies deep within you. This program gives you the golden key. A 2-tape album filled with all the timeless methods you'll need. (PDA-2, $19.95)

The Speaker's Bonus Special

Here's what you get:

The Art of Public Speaking 4-tape album
How to Hold an Audience in the Hollow of Your Hand Book
Anatomy of a Speech Booklet
How Funny Are You? Book
The Art of Greatness 2-tape album

A $89.75 Value for Only $59.95 (PSC-1)

GROWTH UNLIMITED, INC.
36 Fairview
Battle Creek, MI 49017
Toll Free 1-800-441-7676
616-965-2229 Fax: 616-965-4522

Item No.	Description	Quantity	Price Each	Price Total
			Subtotal	
			MI Res, 4% Tax	
			+ 10% Shipping ($3 Minimum)	
	Please find my check or money order enclosed		Total Order	

Charge my VISA ❑ MasterCard ❑ or American Express ❑

Card No:	Expires (Mo/Yr):
Signature:	Tel. No:
Name:	
Address:	
City:	St: Zip:

We guarantee 100% satisfaction on all of our products. If, for any reason, you are not delighted with any of our products, just return them for a 100% refund.

SEND IN YOUR ORDER TODAY!